T0158463

A SHORT HISTORY OF
MODERN IRELAND

Richard Killeen

McGill-Queen's University Press

Montreal & Kingston • Chicago

Gill Books
Hume Avenue
Park West
Dublin 12
www.gillbooks.ie

Gill Books is an imprint of M.H. Gill & Co.

© Richard Killeen 2003
Reprinted 2016

ISBN 978-0-7735-2670-9 (paper)
ISBN 978-0-7735-7174-7 (ePDF)

Index compiled by Kate Duffy

Design by Slick Fish

Printed in Canada on acid-free paper that is
100% ancient forest free (100% post-consumer
recycled), processed chlorine free

A catalogue record is available for this book
from the British Library

1 3 5 4 2

CONTENTS

ACKNOWLEDGMENTS

The publishers are grateful to the following for permission to reproduce copyright illustrations on the following pages:

Gettyimages 4, 110; Leeds Museums and Galleries (Lotherton Hall) UK/Bridgeman Art Gallery 5; National Gallery of Ireland 7, 10, 17, 23, 32, 34, 67, 72; National Library of Ireland 11; The Office of Public Works 13, 15; Denis Mortell 20; Muckross House Research Library (Hilliard Collection) 30; Mark Joyce 33; RTÉ Archive Stills collection 35; Illustrated London News 43; Irish Architectural Archive 51; Popperfoto 58, 93; Mary Evans Picture Library 60; Billy Strickland (INPHO) 77, 119; Trustees of the National Museums & Galleries of Northern Ireland 81; SIPTU 85; National Museum of Ireland 90; Crawford Municipal Art Gallery 92; ESB Art Collection 97; Colman Doyle 100; Felix Rosenstiel's Widow & Son Ltd, London, on behalf of the estate of Sir John Lavery, Trustees of the National Museums & Galleries of Northern Ireland 104; Robert Knudsen, White House/John Fitzgerald Kennedy Library Boston 108; Neil Jarman 113; Eamonn Farrell, Photocall Ireland! 116; Derek Speirs/Report 117.

Despite their best efforts the publishers were unable to trace all copyright holders prior to publication of this book. However, they will make the usual and appropriate arrangements with any who contact them after publication.

1

GATHERING STORM

The English in Ireland

From the time of the Tudor monarchs in the sixteenth century, Ireland had been a security worry for England. In medieval times, England had faced little realistic danger of invasion from continental Europe. From 1550 on, two things changed this. First, advances in shipbuilding technology made naval armadas more formidable. Second, the bitter wars of religion sparked off by the Reformation raised the stakes for all concerned. English fears of the Irish back door were neither hysterical nor misplaced.

Ireland was the only one of the three kingdoms – England (including Wales), Scotland and Ireland – that remained substantially Catholic after the Reformation. Apart from Ulster, where a large number of Anglo-Scots Protestants had been settled in the early seventeenth century following the destruction of the Gaelic lords, the rest of the island resisted reform. The two great Catholic powers of Western Europe, Spain and France, had a potential Catholic beachhead in Ireland.

This made it essential that Ireland be governed in the interests of English security. After the confused series of wars that dominated the Tudor and Stuart eras, it seemed as if the Protestant interest in Ireland had finally triumphed in 1691 at Aughrim, the most decisive battle in Irish history. It meant the defeat of King James II, the last Catholic king of England, by his son-in-law William III and with it the defeat of the Catholic interest in Ireland itself.

For most of the eighteenth century, Ireland was ruled by a tiny Anglican elite – probably no more than 10 per cent of the population. The Ascendancy, as they were later known, were not simply a colonial elite. All *ancien regime* governments were tiny elites: nowhere in Europe was there any notion of popular sovereignty or majority rule, ideas that for most of human history had been thought synonymous with mob rule and

1

anarchy. The Ascendancy thought of themselves as local grandees governing in the king's name, just as their equivalents did in Northumberland or Bavaria or Languedoc. The difference was that Ireland in theory was a separate kingdom sharing a common king with England. At the same time, it was plain that the Ascendancy were – as many of them saw themselves – the English in Ireland. Most Ascendancy families had been settled in Ireland following the Cromwellian confiscations of Catholic lands in the 1650s. As such, they had many of the qualities of a colonial garrison. The Ascendancy was never quite sure what it was. Was it merely the natural ruling class of a separate kingdom? Or a peripheral elite at the margin of a larger Anglo-Irish world? Or a colonial pro-consular bridgehead? There was no unanimous answer to these questions.

Protestants and Catholics

The Ascendancy was exclusively Anglican, that is adherents of the Church of Ireland by law established. The majority of the population outside Ulster was Roman Catholic. The Catholic population was not an ethnic monolith. Its two tributary streams were the Old English (or Norman descendants) and the Gaelic Irish.

The Old English Catholics were similar in kind to other recusant groups at the margins of English life in Reformation times: there were similar patterns of resistance to the Reformation in Northumberland, Lancashire and corners of East Anglia. The Old English dominated life in provincial towns and were generally most numerous in the south and east of the island. The other principal Catholic element was the Gaelic population. These were the descendants of the Celtic peoples who had first settled Ireland from 250 BC onwards, obliterating all trace of the aboriginal peoples they had displaced and establishing a cultural and linguistic homogeneity over the entire island. This homogeneity was disturbed first by the Vikings in the eighth century; then by the Normans in the twelfth; and more thoroughly and, from the Gaelic perspective, disastrously by the Protestant colonists and governors (the New English) in the sixteenth and seventeenth centuries. The New English enterprise culminated in the Cromwellian land confiscations – in which the Old English lost more than the Gaels, simply because they had more to lose – and the creation of the land-owning class that in time became the ascendancy.

The Presbyterians of Ulster comprised a regional sub-group that was to be vital in the making of modern Ireland. After the defeat of the Ulster Gaelic lords in 1603, their former lands were declared forfeit to the crown and were 'planted' by settlers from England and Scotland. All were Protestant. But there was a difference: whereas England had opted for a broadly Lutheran model, Scotland had unambiguously embraced Calvinism. This great fault line in Protestantism created many tensions both within England and between England and Scotland. In Ulster, however, the Presbyterians or Calvinists were a majority among the new settlers. Like the Catholics, they were excluded from the gilded circle of the Anglican elite. In fairness, the degree of exclusion was less – they were Protestant, after all – but the Anglicans had every reason to hold them in suspicion.

If Catholicism represented the enemy without in the form of France, Presbyterianism represented a version of the enemy within. For it was the Calvinist element within the Church of England that had prosecuted the English civil war of the 1640s; that had cut off the king's head; and that had presided over the unloved experiment in Puritan government under Cromwell. Moreover, it was the descendants of the English Puritans who settled North America in disproportionate numbers and who inflicted a humiliating defeat on the English crown by successfully seceding from English control and establishing the independence of the United States. When the story of modern Ireland begins in the 1790s, this was a thrillingly recent event.

Anglican suspicion of Presbyterians was not just theological. They disliked the levelling ideas associated with Calvinism in general: the absence of hierarchy in church government; the governance of the church by elected elders and assemblies. It smacked all too much of a kind of democracy and popular sovereignty. So while not disadvantaged as much as Catholics, the Presbyterians had definite grievances. They were obliged to pay tithes to the Church of Ireland; they felt oppressed by Anglican landlords, and many voted with their feet by emigrating to North America. They were tolerated but not loved.

The storming of the Bastille in Paris, 1789

The United Irishmen

The fall of the Bastille in Paris in July 1789 announced the birth of the modern world. The event was celebrated widely in Ireland, not least in Belfast. For the levelling Presbyterians of Ulster, the French Revolution meant the overthrow of tyranny and superstition. The fundamental importance of the French Revolution lay in its assertion of popular sovereignty. The people, not the monarch, were the supreme sovereign power. Authority flowed upward from the people of the nation rather than downward through the king from God. Thus the nation state replaced the royal state. In the place of the king's domain, the underlying assumption was that all the citizens of the state were stakeholders in a collective enterprise. That enterprise was called the nation and the force of collective will that drove it was nationalism. Nationalism – the assertion that a nation must have its own state grounded in popular sovereignty – is one of the most revolutionary political ideas in world history.

In 1791, the Society of United Irishmen was formed in Belfast. The three principal founders were Samuel Neilson, a Presbyterian who started life as a draper, became a newspaper proprietor and later a revolutionary; Thomas Russell, an Anglican ex-army officer and first librarian of the Linenhall

Library in Belfast; and Theobald Wolfe Tone, a Dublin Anglican barrister and pamphleteer. A sister society was soon established in Dublin. The United Irishmen's declared purpose was to create a non-sectarian version of Irish identity in which confessional allegiance would not matter. Instead citizenship, the shared sense of identity in a civic society, would be the governing principle.

The United Irishmen were Irish but not always united. Some merely wanted parliamentary reform within the existing system; others – influenced by the quickening events in France and the outbreak of the revolutionary wars – an outright overthrow of the system and the establishment of an independent Irish republic. The longer the 1790s went on, the more the republican radicals made the running.

The 1790s was the crucible of modern Ireland. That means two things. First, novel ideas and movements developed that could not have flourished under the *ancien régime* and were implicitly hostile to it. Of these, nationalism and popular sovereignty were the most obvious. Second, however, counter-revolutionary forces developed with strong *ancien régime* continuities. They proved extraordinarily durable. Of these, the most important was the Orange Order.

The Irish House of Commons, 1780

The Order was formed in Co. Armagh in 1795, following a sectarian affray known as the Battle of the Diamond. In this, a Protestant faction called 'the Peep o' Day Boys' scored a victory over a Catholic agrarian secret society called the Defenders. These factions were determinedly traditional and confessional, their causes and concerns a world removed from the educated idealists of the United Irishmen. Following the Boys' victory, they withdrew to a pub in Loughgall, Co. Armagh and formed the Orange Order. From the start, the Order was assertively Protestant, lower class, violent, and inveterately hostile to Catholics. It is significant that it drew most of its early support from the Church of Ireland rather than the Presbyterians, many of whom were much more attracted to French republicanism than Irish confessionalism.

The French are on the sea

On 20 September 1792, the cannonade at Valmy saved the French Revolution. Austrian and Prussian troops under the command of the Duke of Brunswick, part of the First Coalition formed by the European powers against the French Republic, were scattered by an artillery barrage from a hastily assembled French volunteer army. Under their commander, Dumouriez, they consolidated their victory at Jemappes, swept the coalition forces out of north-eastern France, annexed Belgium, threatened the southern Netherlands and occupied parts of the Rhineland including Mainz. The following year, Great Britain joined the coalition. Britain was to be at war with France intermittently for the next twenty-three years.

The war transformed the climate in Ireland. It further radicalised many in the United Irishmen. By 1794, mere parliamentary reform was no longer enough: some were now demanding universal male suffrage, a republic and separation from Britain. The government in London responded in new ways as well. First, they persuaded the Dublin administration to force through a limited measure of parliamentary reform in Ireland, allowing some Catholics the vote for the first time. Some other civil disabilities were also removed. Ascendancy Ireland – both at the Castle and the parliament house – had grave reservations about the Catholic Relief Act of 1793 but it was forced through because Britain's strategic necessity in wartime demanded it.

On the other hand, both the London government and the Irish administration determined to crack down on republicanism. A spy called William Jackson betrayed many members of the Dublin United Irishmen, as a result of which the society was suppressed in the capital. It went underground. Among those betrayed by Jackson was Wolfe Tone.

The entry of the Speaker into the Irish House of Commons

Tone was lucky to escape the scaffold. Instead, he went to the United States and subsequently to France. There, he used his considerable charm and powers of persuasion to press the Irish revolutionary cause on the French government. The result was a massive naval invasion force which gathered at Brest in December 1796. Comprising 43 warships and almost 15,000 crack troops under the command of General Lazare Hoche, it slipped past the Royal Navy convoys sent to engage it and reached Bantry Bay just before Christmas.

Bantry Bay is on the south-west coast of Ireland. The French fleet sailed into this magnificent inlet and immediately struck disaster. The prevailing wind, from the south west, should have blown them up the bay to permit them to berth and disembark the troops. Had they done so, the road to Cork lay open. Cork was the principal city of the south and it and the countryside around were poorly defended. The French would have taken it easily. But they never got ashore.

The wind suddenly swung around to the east and blew a gale. The French could not land and Tone, who was aboard one of the leading ships, expressed his frustration by saying that he could have thrown a biscuit onto the shore, so close were they. On Christmas Eve, Hoche gave the order to cut and run and the remnants of the expedition limped back to Brest. It had been an astonishing escape for England.

The near miss galvanised the government both in London and in Dublin. Pre-emptive defensive measures were taken across the country against suspected United Irishmen and their associates. This often involved great brutality on the part of crown forces. But it seemed to have worked when the leadership of the Leinster Directory of the United Irishmen was betrayed by spies in March 1798. The leading revolutionary figures in Dublin were captured. One, the charismatic Lord Edward FitzGerald – a younger son of the Duke of Leinster – was fatally injured.

The presence of a duke's son in the inner councils of a revolutionary organisation was evidence of the danger to the government posed by the United Irishmen. The Society was by now genuinely revolutionary, espousing a republican civic order in which traditional distinctions of religion, class and caste would be sunk in a common citizenship. The demand was for a civic republic, completely independent of Britain.

With the capture of the Dublin leadership, it seemed that the United Irishmen had been beaten before they had begun. It was not so. Within two months, one of the bloodiest conflicts in Irish history would break out.

2

UNITED KINGDOMS

The rising of 1798

In the heated atmosphere of the spring and summer of 1798, all shades of opinion were being pushed towards ever more polarised positions. Among conservative Protestants, enthusiasm for the Orange Order was growing. The government, using regular troops, yeomanry and militias, redoubled its campaign of torture, house-burnings, arbitrary arrests and summary justice.

Although gravely weakened, the relatively decentralised structure of the United Irishmen was not broken. Moreover, the surviving leadership decided that their best hope lay in an early rebellion. There was no point now in waiting for further French help that might never come, or would come too late.

The 1798 rising broke out on the night of 23–24 May. Mail coaches leaving Dublin were intercepted, the signal for the rising to begin. The United Irishmen belied their name by being organised on a county-by-county basis. Early outbreaks in the counties near Dublin were contained, but the rising in Co. Wexford – in the south-east corner of Ireland – was not. Co. Wexford rose on the afternoon of 26 May, as rumours of massacres and other atrocities in neighbouring counties began to filter through. The command structure of the United organisation in Wexford was interesting: it comprised some liberal Protestant landlords along with well-to-do Catholic tenant farmers and some Catholic priests. Not all Protestants were pro-government; not all Catholics were for rebellion.

When the Wexford rising broke out, the county leadership understood itself to be part of a grand national plan. Its job was to secure the county and await orders. They held the county but the orders never came. The rebellion failed in the surrounding counties, just as it prospered briefly in Wexford. The rebels won a decisive victory against regular crown troops in an affray at Oulart Hill, almost in the middle of the county. In doing so, they demonstrated a degree of discipline and organisation not

Wolfe Tone

normally associated with irregular troops. Wexford, the county town, fell to the rebels on 30 May. They had the county, or most of it, but they were on their own.

They quickly realised that their best hope lay in breaking into neighbouring counties and re-igniting the revolution there. This meant a push to the west, which involved taking New Ross, a market town on the upper tidal reaches of the River Barrow. On 5 June, the United troops laid siege to New Ross. In what was easily the bloodiest action of the rising, the fighting raged back and forth all day, often desperate hand-to-hand stuff in the narrow streets of the town. In the end, the rebels were repulsed.

It was a devastating defeat. Of the original rebel army of about

10,000 men, not more than 3,000 retreated in good order. They lost an immense number of guns and pikes, and all but one of their six artillery pieces. Worse, it meant that they were trapped in Co. Wexford. There would be no break out.

Massacre at Scullabogue

At this moment, there occurred an event that has cast a long shadow. A group of prisoners, almost all of them Protestants and loyalists, who had been rounded up by rebel forces from around the southern part of the county in previous days, were held under armed guard in a barn on a farm at Scullabogue, about 10 kilometres east of New Ross. The farm lay along the defeated rebels' line of retreat. Some of those retreating demanded that the prisoners be executed in retaliation for alleged government atrocities in New Ross. Although the historical evidence for such atrocities is tenuous, it is entirely possible that in the desperate conditions of the battle atrocities may have been committed. At any rate, after initial hesitation, the guards at Scullabogue began to execute the male prisoners by shooting them on the lawn. They then locked the rest, including women and children, in the barn and set it alight. None survived. In all, over 100 people perished at Scullabogue.

The Battle of Vinegar Hill, 1798

Whatever the motivation for this ghastly act, it was a long way removed from the civic ideals of the United Irishmen. The influence of French secular republicanism was new in Ireland, less than a decade old and disproportionately strong in the towns and among the educated and the literate. Sectarian tension between Catholic and Protestant, on the other hand, not only went back 250 years to the Reformation: it had been the defining line of division in Irish public life for all that time. Even on the most generous reading of 1798, it is naïve to suppose that civic republicanism somehow displaced sectarianism during the rebellion. Sectarianism had been there in full measure before '98 and it was there long after. Scullabogue was a sectarian massacre done in the name of a notional Irish republic.

Defeat
After New Ross, the Wexford rebellion was in retreat. The battle of Vinegar Hill, just outside Enniscorthy, and the re-capture of Wexford town by government troops the following day, brought it to an end. The Wexford rising of 1798 lasted less than a month and cost the lives of about 30,000 people, most of them non-combatants. The rising involved what one writer has described as 'a lethal mixture of idealism, sectarianism, agrarianism, revolutionary organisation, state terrorism, mayhem and massacre.'

Meanwhile, a remarkable rising had occurred in the north. In Counties Antrim and Down, United Irish rebels – most of them Presbyterians – took up arms. After some early success, they were decisively defeated at Ballinahinch, Co. Down.

As in Wexford, there was a sectarian undertow. The French Revolution was profoundly anti-Catholic Church, which it regarded as a sink of reaction and superstition. In France itself, the most bitter revolutionary wars were civil wars, especially in the western region of the Vendee, where counter-revolutionary Catholic peasants rose in revolt against the new order. They were crushed with merciless savagery by Paris. They had rebelled in the names of throne and altar, and it seemed to all supporters of the Revolution that Catholicism was an enemy. Certainly, the papacy was bitterly opposed to the Revolution from the first and much of subsequent French history was a contest between republican secularism and reactionary clericalism. All this made the principles of the French Revolution perhaps too congenial to Presbyterian Ulster, where its anti-Catholicism was easily compatible with ancient local sentiment. It certainly militated against the fullest embrace of the United Irish ideal of Protestant, Catholic and Dissenter joined in a common citizenship. It is significant that the Ulster rebellion was centred in the two eastern counties of Down and Antrim, the counties with the fewest number of Catholics and therefore with the least sectarian tension: ironically, the minimal Catholic numbers created the oxygen for republican sentiment to thrive. In neighbouring Co. Armagh, with its volatile balance of populations, the appeal of the United Irishmen was diminished. That of the Orange Order and its Catholic analogue, the Defenders, was maximised.

The Battle of Ballinahinch in Co. Down, 1798

With the government victories at Vinegar Hill, Wexford and Ballinahinch, it seemed that the brief efflorescence of republican separatism in Ireland had been snuffed out. Not quite: there was a double coda. First, a small French expedition under General Humbert arrived in the far west, in Co. Mayo, in August, picked up local support and lasted six weeks before the inevitable surrender. Finally, Wolfe Tone returned to Ireland as part of another small French fleet. Wearing the uniform of a French officer, he was arrested and taken to Dublin where he committed suicide rather than be hanged for treason.

The Act of Union 1801

The United Irish rebellions had been intended to deliver a non-sectarian Irish republic. Their actual outcome resulted in a union of the kingdoms of Britain and Ireland in a single state, and one moreover where profound sectarian antagonism was the order of the day. The sectarian excesses in Wexford – however unrepresentative of the broad United leadership in the county – had none the less sent shock waves through Protestant Ireland and certainly contributed to the failure of the Ulster rebellion to spread beyond two counties.

The Act of Union of 1801 abolished the kingdom of Ireland as a separate entity. With it went the Irish parliament, that bastion resistant to the last against parliamentary reform. The United Kingdom was born and with it the Union Jack, uniting the crosses of SS George, Andrew and Patrick.

Repeal of the union would dominate Irish political life in the nineteenth century. It was to be the central demand of Irish nationalism, which would develop into an overwhelmingly Catholic project. It was ironic, therefore, that most Catholic opinion in 1800 welcomed the union. In the first place, it meant the end of the unreformed and corrupt parliament of the Protestant ascendancy. In the second place, it was to be accompanied by a measure of Catholic Emancipation. Locked in a deadly struggle with France, William Pitt, the British prime minister, recognised the need to avoid a disaffected population in Ireland. Catholics had suffered under a series of Penal Laws since the 1690s. Catholic political power was curbed by the denial of property rights; entry to parliament or the legal profession was barred; and Catholics could not keep their own schools. The relief measures now proposed would essentially grant Catholics full parliamentary rights in return for a government veto on Catholic episcopal appointments. The Catholic hierarchy conducted discussions with the London government in this broad context.

It would be easier to grant full political rights to Catholics in the overall Protestant context of a union parliament. In a purely Irish context, however, Catholic political rights would be a direct threat to Protestant hegemony.

The plan foundered on the inflexible opposition of the king. George III regarded such concessions as a violation of his coronation oath, which pledged to uphold the Protestant nature of the state. Like a lot of stupid people, it took a great deal to get an idea into the king's head but once there, there was no shifting it. The failure to couple Catholic Emancipation with the union was regarded as a betrayal by Irish Catholic opinion, one that blighted relations between Catholics and the new order from the start.

Catholic self-consciousness

The new regime meant that Ireland was no longer a separate kingdom but an integral part of the British state. In one respect, however, there was little change. The Irish administrative machinery remained not just a Protestant preserve, but increasingly an Orange one. The horrors of 1798 seized the imagination of many Irish Protestants, who did what people

St Patrick's Day Parade at Dublin Castle

everywhere do when they feel threatened and vulnerable. They sought refuge in a more radical and defensive statement of their position. In the Protestant community, the ultras were able to say to the liberals: we told you so. And thus the ultras controlled Dublin Castle, the seat of British administration in Ireland, in the early years of the union.

The practical effect was to underscore the oppositional bitterness between Protestant and Catholic in Ireland. Liberal Protestants were marginalised as a group. Meanwhile, in the first two decades of the new century, a sea-change was occurring among the Catholics which was to be the decisive social and intellectual shift in nineteenth-century Ireland. The idea of the modern Irish nation was being born.

The principles of republican government, independence and popular sovereignty had all been asserted in 1798. This was the work of a political elite, many of them Protestant radicals intoxicated by the revolutionary fervour coming from France. This new ideal of a civic order, indifferent to religion, was severely damaged by the sectarian outrages in Wexford. Its last aftershock, the failed insurrection of Robert Emmet in Dublin in 1803, also resulted in unintended tragedy. It was quickly snuffed out and was in fact little more than an affray, but one which claimed the life of Lord Kilwarden, the Lord Chief Justice, a notably liberal judge. The irony was that Kilwarden's birth name was Arthur Wolfe. He was a member of the family for whom Wolfe Tone had been named (Tone's father had been a tenant on the Wolfe estate) and he himself had used his influence to help save Tone's life back in 1794 when Tone's activities had been betrayed to the government. After a speech from the dock that still resonates in Irish history, Emmet was hanged.

In place of civic republicanism, the older tradition of Catholic self-consciousness re-asserted itself. But now an embryonic national consciousness began to form within it. Gaelic Ireland – to take the larger element in the Catholic community – had long had a cultural unity while being bitterly divided politically. Only as Catholics began to believe that what they had in common was paramount and what divided them was of little consequence did the community begin to develop a national self-consciousness. It is the key process in the birth of nationalism and by the 1880s it was the most potent force in Irish life. Why did it happen, and why did it happen when it did?

First, there was the intellectual revolution: the idea of popular sovereignty which provided a template into which ideas that had hitherto been diffuse could now cohere.

Second, there was the rise of a Catholic middle class. This too was crucial. All nations require a leadership element to focus their emerging national consciousness. In every European case – in Poland, Bohemia, Hungary, Germany – the people who made the running were always the same: lawyers, doctors, professors, younger sons of minor gentry. These were educated people, ambitious but usually frustrated by institutional or political impediment to their advance. These impediments were invariably embedded deep in the structures of the old regime.

A Bianconi car in 1856

Third, there was the gradual destruction of distance which helped to create a sense of national as distinct from local community. Better roads and coach services and canals were a beginning, but above all it was the coming of the railways that made this possible. It created a distribution network for goods and services nationally. It created a national press, because it facilitated the countrywide distribution of newspapers published in Dublin. By the second half of the century, there was a national community in the sense that matters of common national interest had a means of common expression. The Catholics of Antrim were no longer remote from those of Kerry: they no longer shared just a common culture, but now had common political aspirations as well. And the first of those aspirations was fair play for the Catholic community, which began with the demand for Catholic Emancipation. Later, nationalism demanded the repeal of the union; later, after the Famine, it re-cast this demand in the form of the home rule movement; finally, it asserted itself in arms and formulated the demand for full independence from Britain.

The self-conscious community of Irish Catholics began its life in the first two decades of the nineteenth century, in the era of Orange administrative dominance. The sense of betrayal over Catholic Emancipation went deep. It was this cause that became the focus of Catholic aspiration. Moreover, it found a leader and organiser of genius. His name was Daniel O'Connell.

3

LIBERATOR

The *ancien régime* and the radicals

Daniel O'Connell was the scion of a minor Gaelic aristocratic family from Co. Kerry. His background was classically part of that hidden Ireland of the *ancien régime*. The O'Connells had survived and prospered in a modest way in their remote coastal fastness, not scrupling to trade in smuggled goods if necessary. The young Daniel was sent to the Jesuit schools in Saint-Omer and Douai to be educated. O'Connell arrived there in 1791 and witnessed at first hand enough of the violence associated with the French Revolution to give him a lifelong aversion to political violence in general. He later studied law in London.

He was one of the first generation of Catholics allowed to practise law under the terms of one of the Relief Acts that ended the Penal Laws. He qualified in 1798, the year of rebellion. He was a member of a lawyers' reserve militia mobilised to defend Dublin against a threatened United Irish attack that never materialised. He went on to practise on the Munster circuit, made and spent fortunes and married happily.

He was drawn to political prominence from 1808 on by the veto controversy. The proponents of Catholic Emancipation assumed that – as at the time of the union – the Catholic hierarchy would concede to the British government a veto on Irish episcopal appointments as a *quid pro quo* for Emancipation. The demand for a veto of some sort had been there since the Catholic Church had started to emerge from the wilderness years of the Penal Laws in the last quarter of the eighteenth century with an institutional vigour that astonished and dismayed London. The proposed veto was intended to exercise at least some degree of negative control over the leadership of this potentially dangerous body. Moreover, it was the norm in many parts of Europe: the Protestant kings of Prussia exercised a veto over the appointment of bishops to the Catholic Church in Poland, for example.

The monument to Daniel O'Connell in Dublin

The more radical, middle-class faction among Irish Catholic activists was unimpressed by Prussia or anywhere else. They were adamant in opposition to the veto. An older, more aristocratic leadership – both among the hierarchy and the laity – was open to the possibility but they were overborne. The controversy rumbled on all through the 1810s. In part, the anti-vetoists were representing a generational change, in part a class one: what was significant was the exceptional vigour with which they argued for the absolutely free-standing autonomy of the Catholic community and its church.

This was part of the great change that was quietly transforming Irish Catholicism. The growing self-consciousness of the community *as a community* marked the change. The aristocratic old order was prepared to accommodate itself to the state, however reluctantly, in a typically *ancien régime* way. The radicals were not. They were thinking not of the state but of the nation. The passions aroused by the veto question split Irish Catholics bitterly and made any united political action on Emancipation impossible until the wounds had healed in the 1820s.

The Catholic community in the south-east

The Catholic Church had suffered the disabilities of the Penal Laws for most of the eighteenth century. It emerged into the new century in remarkably fine shape, considering the rigours of the old one. All the dioceses had bishops in residence, there were numerous priests, the Irish church was in full communion with Rome and while many peasant practices persisted which the clergy deplored as superstitious, there was a movement towards doctrinal and liturgical orthodoxy which advanced steadily as time went on.

The church was strongest where the community was strongest. One of the striking things about the church in the early nineteenth century was its regional disparities. In the impoverished west of Ireland, it still remained a pre-modern peasant body. But in the south-east, in the rich river valleys and towns where the Old English Catholic middle class had survived the bad days in good order – trading, farming, maintaining family networks through inter-marriage, educating their sons in Catholic countries abroad – the church was strong. The simplest way to illustrate this is to look at the foundation dates of Catholic institutions. The cathedral in Waterford – a fine neo-classical building, product of a self-confident, wealthy community, not at all the impoverished, humiliated people of folk-memory – dates from 1793. The same year saw the opening of what is now Carlow College and was then the first post-penal era institution of higher learning for Catholics in the country. The adjacent cathedral was begun in 1828, as was the parish church in Dungarvan, Co. Waterford. In nearby Youghal, Co. Cork, the parish church was built in 1796 in mock-Anglican style. These are all very early foundation dates: most of the institutional revival of Catholicism – especially in church building – came in the second half of the nineteenth century.

The Catholic elite of the south-east, roughly east of a line from Dublin to Cork, were a generation or two ahead of the rest of their co-religionists in terms of their social cohesion, wealth and influence. It is no coincidence that so many leading figures in the nineteenth-century hierarchy come disproportionately from this region.

Similarly, it is remarkable how many of O'Connell's political lieutenants in the campaign for Emancipation came from the south-east. Thomas Wyse from Co. Waterford, who married a Bonaparte, was one such. Another was Richard Lalor Sheil from Co. Kilkenny. Denys Scully was from Kilfeakle, Co. Tipperary. All were hugely influential in their time; all came from wealthy backgrounds. Sheil and Scully were lawyers.

Irish nationalism, or at least the version of it that was to dominate the history of the island for the next 150 years or so, first developed among the privileged community of Catholics in the south-east. Their project was overtly confessional, the relief of remaining religious disabilities through the winning of Catholic Emancipation. Thereafter, they looked for repeal of the union, confident in the superiority of Catholic numbers.

The Catholic Association

In 1823, Daniel O'Connell founded the Catholic Association. It was just the latest in a series of such associations that had been formed in the ten years or so since the veto controversy was at its height. None had prospered. Like the others, this new association was composed of the usual middle-class elite: the subscription was a guinea a year, about six months' rent for a middling farmer. A year later, in March 1824, a new category of associate member was launched at the cost of a penny a month, the so-called 'Catholic rent'.

It transformed the association. More than that, it transformed the entire history of Ireland. It announced the arrival of the politics of mass mobilisation, the first such populist movement in Europe. It took the government a further year to suppress the association. By then, the rent had raised about £17,000 for the association; significantly, nearly all of this came from Leinster and Munster. In addition, the new association had begun the creation of a national network of local committees and activists. The simplest way of doing this was to tap into the one existing organisational structure that was tailor-made for the purpose: the Catholic parish system.

A mass meeting of the Catholic Association in Dublin

When the Catholic Association was suppressed in 1825, O'Connell responded by forming the New Catholic Association and re-starting the rent. In 1826, there was a general election. Although Catholics were not permitted to sit in parliament, many liberal Protestants stood in support of the Catholic Association. The key contest was in Co. Waterford, in the heartland of advanced Catholic consciousness.

The electorate was small. Its key element was the forty-shilling freeholders, that is tenants whose holding was valued at £2 (or 40 shillings) per annum after rents and other charges had been paid. Traditionally the forty-shilling freeholders had been creatures of their landlords: there was no secret ballot and each man had to declare his choice publicly. It was generally an unwise tenant who voted against his landlord's wishes.

The landlord in question was the Marquis of Waterford, head of the powerful Beresford family. The Tory candidate was his son, Lord George Thomas Beresford. Opposing Beresford was a young liberal landlord, Villiers Stuart, who won. The settled pattern of generations was broken: the forty-shilling freeholders abandoned the Beresfords and embraced the candidate supported by the Catholic Association. It was a transfer of loyalty on a seismic scale and the first visible sign of the pattern that marked the advance of Irish nationalism: the deference of the *ancien régime* was replaced by Catholic communal solidarity.

Catholic Emancipation

The pattern was repeated in the tumultuous by-election in Clare in 1828, when O'Connell himself stood, although barred from entering parliament. After a contest drenched in the most uncompromising sectarian rhetoric – O'Connell knew his market – he won. Faced with outright electoral revolt in Ireland, and the implicit threat of something worse, the Tory government of Wellington and Peel capitulated in 1829. Catholic Emancipation was granted: Catholics could now sit in parliament; hold office; and become judges. The price extracted to save some of the government's face was the raising of the franchise threshold in Ireland from forty shillings (£2) to £10. Thus the forty-shilling freeholders, who won Catholic Emancipation, were disenfranchised for their pains – at least for the moment.

It was O'Connell's greatest hour. He was fifty-four years old and beyond question the dominant figure in Irish life. To his contemporaries, he was a mixture of hero and enigma. He had titanic energy and organising ability; a sulphurous temper; torrential eloquence; vast reservoirs of charm. He was a genuine liberal in many respects, as his parliamentary career was to prove – he was a free trader and anti-slaver at a time when these were litmus tests of liberalism – yet he led a movement that was nakedly confessional. His political organisation was based on the Catholic parishes and with the parishes came the priests. O'Connell stands accused of introducing the priests into Irish politics. He might have replied that he simply used the most practical means to hand and that, after all, the confessional rivalry between Protestant and Catholic was the decisive line of division in Irish life.

It was. The problem for O'Connell was that Ireland was not all Catholic. The three provinces of Leinster, Munster and Connacht were overwhelmingly so. But the northern province, Ulster, was not.

Resistance from Ulster

Ulster had a Protestant majority. It was not a united community. Tensions between members of the established Church of Ireland (Anglican), mainly of English descent, and the Presbyterians of Scots descent were very marked. The liberal impulse in Presbyterianism, with its instinct for democracy, had found expression in 1798. Although much chastened thereafter, it took a long time for this liberal Presbyterian tradition to die. But by 1830 it was increasingly under challenge.

Presbyterianism, with its highly literate congregations, was a fertile ground for theological disputation. In the first half of the nineteenth century, conservative and orthodox subscribers to the Westminster Confession of Faith – the foundation document of the Church of Scotland – gradually marginalised the so-called non-subscribers within Ulster. In broad political terms, it was a victory for conservatives and evangelicals over those of a more liberal, accommodating temper.

The one thing that united all Ulster Protestants, whether Church of Ireland or any shade of Presbyterian, was suspicion and dislike of Catholics. The antagonism ran long and deep, right back to original Plantation days and it had never abated. It was no coincidence that the swing to conservatism in Presbyterianism coincided with the growing advance of Catholic interests under O'Connell.

As part of his campaign to organise nationally, O'Connell looked towards Ulster. Like Connacht, but for different reasons, it was not nearly as promising territory as the southern provinces. There was no self-confident Catholic middle class around which a mass movement could form and which would provide leadership for it. Moreover, there was a Protestant majority many of whom were enthusiastic Orange partisans. The point was made with some vigour in September 1828.

O'Connell approved an initiative by one of his more maverick allies, Honest Jack Lawless, to try to extend the reach of the Catholic Association to Ulster. This initiative was known by the revealing title of 'the invasion of Ulster', Honest Jack's own formulation. He led a large crowd north but was repulsed by a formidable gathering of Orangemen in Ballybay, Co. Monaghan. It was the first town on the southern reaches of Ulster where Protestants felt confident enough to muster in serious numbers. Lawless wisely backed off. Humiliatingly, that was as far as things went for the 'invasion' force: in the face of the first concentrated Ulster Protestant resistance to a nationalist initiative, all they could do was to retreat.

It was a portent. Resistance – bringing weight of numbers to bear in concentrated form – became the essence of the Ulster Protestant position as the nineteenth century wore on. There were lots of Ulster Protestants; they were concentrated in a small area; they were not going anywhere and there was no shifting them.

By the 1830s, the broad pattern of modern Irish history was in place. The Catholic community had realised its collective self-image and embarked on its political project. What began as a campaign to relieve Catholic disabilities gradually developed first into a campaign for Irish autonomy within the United Kingdom and later into a demand for outright independence.

The advance of the Irish nationalist project is interesting. It was not unique in Europe but its methods were. The contrast with Polish nationalism makes the point nicely. The Poles had seen their country dismembered in the Three Partitions and divided between Russia, Prussia and the Habsburgs. Their nineteenth-century nationalist movement found itself facing three states with no tradition of representative government. So the leadership of Polish nationalism embarked on what they called 'organic work': educating the people in their history and folklore; artists and writers producing didactic work on Polish themes; economic development; movements for social cohesion. The kind of people who led this organic work were from the same sort of social background as O'Connell's lieutenants in Ireland: people like Wyse, Sheil, Scully and Lawless. But where the Poles directed their energies to what might broadly be called cultural and economic development, the Irish chose politics. They did so because the country of which they were a part, the United Kingdom, had one of the longest continuous traditions of representative government in Europe. Britain was no democracy – not yet – but it did possess representative institutions, of which the most important was the House of Commons. It meant that Irish nationalism had a representative forum in which to express itself from the start: from 1829 to 1914, the House of Commons in London was the focus of all constitutional nationalist effort. In Poland, organic work represented the only nationalist alternative to insurrection. In Ireland, it was politics. From the beginning, Irish nationalism was about numbers and representation; it was about incremental change and the practical politics of the here and now; it was populist. Thus the emphasis on organisation and mobilisation, on ward politics, and the impatience with theory. Irish populist politics first developed under O'Connell. It was perfected later in the century under Parnell. It has been exported wherever the Irish diaspora has gone in numbers and has given the world, among other things, Tammany Hall and much of the Democratic Party in the USA; a significant element of the Labour Party and trade union movement in Britain; and a substantial part of the Labor Party and trade union movement in Australia. All this made Irish nationalism unusual in a European context. In Ireland, politics came first and culture followed. In comparable continental countries, it tended to be the other way around. This may explain why, in the 1920s and '30s, so many of the new states in Europe turned towards various forms of authoritarian government, while Ireland – despite the bitterness of the civil war divide – did not. Politics had become second nature to Irish nationalists. With its internal logic of compromise, the political process provided the normal means of settling great public issues. When you have a legitimate parliament, you have no need for a Man on a White Horse.

4

UNDER THE VOLCANO

O'Connell-Whig Alliance

With Catholic Emancipation won, O'Connell entered parliament in London and gradually formed a loose group of supporters around him. This was not a party in any modern sense, with all the discipline and regimentation that term implies. Until the fall of Wellington and Peel in 1832, he had little parliamentary leverage, but the accession of the Whigs to power in that year improved the position. O'Connell felt much closer to the Whigs, with their generally more liberal inclinations, than he possibly could to the royalist and reactionary Tories – especially given the latter's Orange allies in Ireland.

O'Connell reached an understanding with the Whigs which brought some immediate benefits. The long-running sore of the tithe question was settled. Tithes had been payable either in cash or kind for the upkeep of the clergy of the established Church of Ireland, whose congregations constituted barely 10 per cent of the entire Irish population. Tithes had always been resented and had been the proximate cause of sporadic campaigns of agrarian violence ever since the 1760s. These campaigns had escalated in the early 1830s, resulting in serious violence in the countryside. In general, attempts to enforce payment – or worse, to distrain goods for non-payment, met with fierce resistance. The settlement of this issue removed one of the most potent sources of social unrest in Ireland.

Other reforms effected by the O'Connell-Whig alliance included the modernisation of the archaic system of municipal government by widening the franchise. Among other things, it allowed O'Connell to become the first Catholic lord mayor of Dublin for 150 years. A Poor Law enacted in 1838 provided a minimal structure of poor relief in what was still a desperately poor country. The Irish administration was increasingly staffed by Catholics and liberal Protestants, weakening the Orange grip on Dublin Castle. The under-secretary (head of the Irish civil service), Thomas Drummond, famously reminded Irish landlords that 'property has its duties as well as its rights', not the sort of sentiment normally expected from the Castle. The establishment of the Irish Constabulary (the 'Royal' prefix came later, for services rendered in helping to put down the Fenian insurrection of 1867) and the Dublin Metropolitan Police in 1836 put Irish law enforcement on a modern footing.

Campaign for repeal of the union

But the real political action gradually came to focus not on these worthy reforms but on the larger constitutional issue. O'Connell launched a campaign for the repeal of the union of 1801 and the restoration of a parliament in Dublin. As the Whig government began to run out of steam, O'Connell reckoned that the potential for further reforming concessions was lessening by the day. With the return of the Tories under his old adversary Peel in 1841, the possibility vanished altogether.

O'Connell could therefore go for broke. He revived the methods that had stood him in such good stead in the Emancipation campaign: a national organisation, again leaning heavily on Catholic parish structures, complemented by fund-raising and propaganda. To this potent brew he added a new element, the so-called 'monster meeting'.

Monster meetings were enormous public gatherings designed to show the formidable powers of organisation and control that O'Connell exercised over the people. They aimed to intimidate the government by sheer weight of numbers and by the implicit threat of public disorder on a massive scale. The meetings were organised at historic sites like Tara, Co. Meath and were always addressed by O'Connell.

Three things contributed to the failure of the repeal agitation. First, the Catholic hierarchy, although sympathetic, did not feel that repeal was as urgent a measure as Emancipation had been and did not throw their weight behind it to the same degree. Second, there was no body of sympathetic opinion in England as there had been in the earlier campaign. Third, Peel exploited this knowledge to take a stand against O'Connell. When a monster meeting was announced for the Dublin suburb of Clontarf – site of a famous battle against the Vikings in 1014 – the government banned it. Fearing violence, which he loathed, O'Connell backed down and abandoned the meeting.

The railway revolution

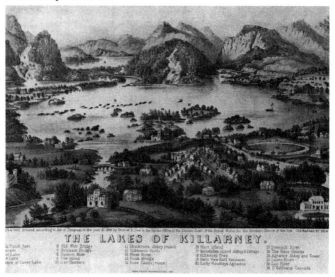

An American poster of 1868 advertising the Lakes of Killarney, whose pre-eminent position as a tourist destination was a consequence of railway development

The first Irish railway, the Dublin & Kingstown, opened in December 1834. Within twenty years Dublin was connected to Belfast, Cork and Galway and there were a host of minor lines, radiating from these centres, either planned or already in place. The expansion of the Irish railway system continued up to the 1920s, when road transport began to supplant it. The railways were crucial in the process of consolidating national consciousness. A journey like that from Dublin to Cork, which had taken two days by coach, was reduced to seven hours in 1849 and four hours by 1887. It was the greatest advance in mobility in human history and it led to all sorts of unanticipated consequences. It made possible the creation of a genuinely national press, by providing a distribution mechanism from

Dublin. Thus, people at either end of the island could read the same newspaper on the same day. Likewise, it made the distribution of everything from tinned foods to beer easier and helped to create a national retail economy. It offered opportunities for leisure travel to tens of thousands to whom it was previously denied: the great Victorian 'watering places' – such seaside resorts as Bray, Tramore and Clifden – all owe their origins to the railway, as does Killarney as the centre of Irish tourism. The French Revolution may have created the idea of the nation state, but the railways gave it a physical reality. The transport revolution turned a notional community into a national one. Before the railway, people in Co. Antrim had more contact with Argyll than with Kerry. The railway connected people in a way that gave physical expression to their underlying cultural unity. Dublin's position as the nodal point in the railway system consolidated it as a national rather than just a colonial capital.

The anglicisation of Ireland

The death of languages is a melancholy feature of modernity: the standard speech of metropolitan elites overwhelms regional dialects and marginal languages. As modern states form themselves, the metropolitan language of commerce, law, administration and journalism exercises a powerful hold. An ambitious provincial, anxious to make a career in business, law or the civil service, must learn the language of power. The metropolitan explosion of newspapers and books in nineteenth-century Europe reinforced the tendency. In the twentieth century, radio, television and the internet accelerated it further. Regional speech – both patois and minority languages – suffered accordingly. Ireland has been no exception to this process.

English had obviously been the language of the Ascendancy in Ireland in the eighteenth century. But the vast majority of the Irish population in 1800 spoke Irish, either as the sole vernacular or bilingually. By the mid-1830s, it was estimated that about 50 per cent of the population spoke the old language. The 1851 census gave a figure of 1.5 million people – less than a quarter of the whole – who spoke only Irish. This precipitate decline obviously reflects the devastating effects of the Famine. It was a decline that has continued unabated to the present day. But it is important to observe that the Famine merely accelerated a pre-existing pattern of decline.

Daniel O'Connell's first language had been Irish. As an adult, he was a champion of Catholic rights, the effective developer of what became the mainstream nationalist tradition, but he was indifferent to the Irish language to the point of hostility. This indifference was rooted in a utilitarian view of language itself. In 1833, admitting that the use of Irish was diminishing among the peasantry, he observed that 'the superior utility of the English tongue, as the medium of all modern communication, is so great, that I can witness without a sigh the gradual disuse of Irish'. This might be the voice of any ambitious provincial in Europe in the age before the idea of cultural nationalism established its dominance.

The anglicisation of Ireland is perhaps the key cultural development of the entire nineteenth century. There was a great irony in all this: just as Ireland was moving farther from England politically, it was drawing closer to it culturally. By the mid-century, the immense prestige of an England approaching the apogee of her power – the workshop of the world, rich beyond

A nineteenth-century kitchen interior

Thomas Davis' statue in College Green, Dublin

the dreams of earlier generations – had a powerful gravitational pull for all within its orbit.

The Young Irelanders

On 15 October 1842, the first edition of *The Nation* appeared in Dublin. The founders were Charles Gavan Duffy, a self-educated journalist; John Blake Dillon, a barrister; and Thomas Davis, barrister and minor poet. All were provincials from middle-class backgrounds: Dillon and Duffy were the sons of shopkeepers, Davis of an army surgeon.

The Nation was an astonishing success, at one point in the 1840s claiming a readership of almost 250,000. It was a radical nationalist paper. Although it supported O'Connell's repeal campaign, its emphasis was different to his. Where O'Connell was basically utilitarian in temperament, *The Nation* was Romantic. The Romantic movement had swept across Europe in the previous generation in reaction to the cool, calculating classicism of the Enlightenment. The surging music of Beethoven, the lyrical exuberance of Wordsworth and Byron, the sublime landscapes of Caspar David Friedrich: all were part of a common sensibility. This was what *The Nation* tapped into.

In political terms, Young Ireland – as the group clustered

Wake for a drowned child on the Aran islands

around *The Nation* became known – introduced a different
strain of nationalist thought to Ireland. It was heavily influenced
by German Romanticism as mediated through the work of the
Scottish writer Thomas Carlyle. The nation was defined less in
legal terms – popular sovereignty and the will of the people –
than in cultural. It was literary – Davis was the pre-eminent
popular poet of his day and some of his poems are still popular
in ballad form – and it wished to promote a distinctively
national literature. It was the first national movement to propose
a revival of the Irish language. It emphasised the iconography of
modern Irish nationalism: the harps and shamrocks, round
towers and Irish wolfhounds, and introduced the tricolour flag.
One of the Young Irelanders, Thomas Francis Meagher, brought
the green, white and orange flag back from Paris in 1848. It was
an obvious imitation of the French revolutionary *tricoleur*.

In ordinary political terms, Young Ireland was a repeal ginger
group but relations between them and O'Connell were tense. In
part, they represented a generational challenge to the elderly
leader. But there was more than that. O'Connell's utilitarianism
had led him to accept, however reluctantly, a confessional
context for his campaigns. His was substantially a Catholic
movement. Young Ireland, with its emphasis on culture,

proposed a more inclusive definition of nationality. It was rooted in different soil to the non-sectarianism of the United Irishmen in the 1790s but the fruits were very similar. O'Connell emphasised the practical politics of Catholic numbers, Young Ireland the idealist politics of a nation in which common citizenship would override religious differences.

In 1845, the British government established three universities in Ireland, the so-called Queen's Colleges, at Belfast, Cork and Galway. They were founded on a strictly non-sectarian basis. No state funding was provided for the support of chairs of theology, although private endowments were not forbidden. The campaign for a Catholic university had been a major demand from O'Connell and the hierarchy and the British hoped that the Queen's Colleges would satisfy the demand. Not so. O'Connell and the bishops denounced the 'godless colleges' and re-doubled their campaign for a specifically Catholic institution in which the church, not the state, would hold the reins.

The canals revolutionised transport in the early nineteenth century

Young Ireland welcomed the Queen's Colleges as a major step forward. They recoiled from a confessionalism that effectively coupled Irish identity with Catholicism. Davis himself was a Protestant. There was a terrible irony here: O'Connell's populism was democratic; Young Ireland's idealism was not. It was an elite subset of nationalism with shallow roots among the people, for all the popularity of *The Nation*.

This fault line in Irish nationalism would reappear. In the meantime, Davis died tragically young in 1845. O'Connell himself, his prestige reduced since the climb-down at Clontarf and in ever declining health, would die in January 1847. And Ireland all unknowing stood on the brink of the greatest natural catastrophe in her history.

5

FAMINE

Demography and diet

The first reliable Irish census took place in 1841. It showed a population of just over 8 million people. Prior to 1760, the total Irish population had probably been less than 2.5 million.

The astonishing rise in the Irish population in the century before the Famine was remarked on by all contemporaries. It was accounted for by a number of factors: the widespread introduction of the easily cultivated and nutritious potato, which replaced grain as the staple diet of the poor; economic expansion, especially in agriculture, which raced ahead in the years of the Revolutionary Wars as Ireland helped to provision the British army; early marriages with high fertility rates; lower infant mortality; endless sub-division of tiny holdings.

Although most Irish people were poor, the rich limestone lands of the south and east supported a vigorous commercial agriculture in grain and cattle. Ireland remained a net exporter of food in pre-famine years: it is estimated that about two million people in Britain were fed with produce imported from Ireland. On the other hand, the poorer regions were wretched. In Connacht, the poorest province, 64 per cent of all farms were five acres or less. This was a subsistence economy with a vengeance. In general, the pattern of small holdings, rural overcrowding, severe poverty and lack of capital was more pronounced as one went further north and west.

The reliance on a single crop, the potato, had obvious risks in the event of crop failure or – the more common hazard – a smaller harvest than expected, which would mean some lean months in the coming year. The advantage of potatoes, however, was their exceptional nutritional value. The diet of the pre-Famine Irish poor, buttermilk and potatoes, was monotonous but healthy. Visitors commented with surprise on the physique of the Irish rural poor, comparing it favourably with that of their equivalents in richer countries.

Other advantages included the ease with which potatoes could be cultivated – too easily, said the critics – and their ability to flourish on marginal land otherwise unsuitable for tillage. There is no doubt that the potato monoculture in the poorer parts of Ireland discouraged the introduction of commercial agriculture. The few improving landlords who tried this met with fierce resistance. Commercial agriculture meant, among other things, the enclosure of land previously worked in common. The so-called rundale system of co-operative farming, in which long strips of land were farmed by extended families, was wonderfully fair in ensuring that no family member had a monopoly on the best land. Everyone got more or less the same share of good and bad land. This was socially cohesive and economically insane: it was a guarantee of low yields and offered no incentive to innovate or improve.

The great exception to this general picture was Ulster. Not only was reliance on the potato less than in the other three provinces, there was a thriving flax and linen industry in place since the late eighteenth century. Agriculture was more varied than elsewhere, and the domestic employment offered by linen weaving supplemented farm incomes. Moreover, the finishing and marketing of linen products was concentrated in Belfast, where it was the largest source of early industrial employment. In the 1830s, the first stirrings of the Industrial Revolution were already visible in Belfast. The fact that industry roared ahead in Belfast and much of Ulster during the nineteenth century and failed to do so in the three southern provinces was one of the most significant developments in the story of modern Ireland.

The potato blight

In June 1845, a new and mysterious potato blight appeared for the first time in Europe, in Belgium. By September, it had made its way to Ireland. It resulted in the loss of about one-third of the Irish potato harvest that year. It was a crisis but not a disaster. The blight had appeared late in the year and much of

Children during the Famine

the crop was already harvested when it struck. Even so, the failure of the staple crop on such a scale created a major social problem. It was not unprecedented. There had been partial failures of the crop in every decade of the nineteenth century. The difference was – although no one knew it at the time – that this was a new, virulent and utterly mysterious kind of blight.

The Tory government of Sir Robert Peel responded promptly. Peel had been chief secretary of Ireland from 1812 to 1818 and had provided £250,000 for the relief of distress during food shortages in 1817, in the course of which about 50,000 people had died. Although a Tory and a bitter opponent of O'Connell, he was a realist and it was he who finally introduced the legislation for the Catholic Emancipation Act of 1829.

In November 1845, Peel's government spent £100,000 on buying and distributing Indian corn, i.e. maize, from the United States. It set up a commission to study the causes of the blight and instituted a series of public works which provided subsistence wages for the poor. Peel was a free trader but not an ideologue. Government assistance of this kind was contrary to the principles of free trade, which believed that the self-regulating internal logic of the economic system could only be distorted by government interference. None the less, Peel's government *did* intervene strongly and promptly in the face of such an urgent crisis.

In the summer of 1846, however, the Tory government fell. Ironically, its defeat came as a result of its own success in forcing through the repeal of the Corn Laws. These laws, the great symbolic target of all free traders for a generation, had placed restrictions on the importation of grain into the United Kingdom and had had the effect of acting as a kind of hidden subsidy to large landed interests.

The new Whig government was led by Lord John Russell. It was much more doctrinaire in its espousal of free trade principles and instinctively less likely than Peel had been to bend them or otherwise trim them in the face of circumstance. This had serious consequences in Ireland, for there was a wholesale failure of the potato crop in the summer of 1846. The blight re-appeared earlier that year, before any harvesting could begin. This was the real beginning of the Great Famine.

A heartless response

The distress of the previous year had clearly left parts of the population in a poor position to cope with the shattering effects of total potato failure. The response of the Whig government in London was to reduce grain importation into Ireland and to attempt to run down public works schemes. Despite this, almost 500,000 desperate people were employed in such public works by the end of 1846 and nearly half as many again three months later. Contrary to its own instincts, the government established soup kitchens to feed the people in 1847 but its heart was not in it and they were closed down again at the end of that disastrous year.

Why did the government respond in such a cold-blooded way? It was an article of faith in Westminster that Ireland was a social and economic mess. Its landlords were feckless and reactionary, not given to the sort of modernising improvements that had transformed English agriculture. The tenants were seen as a slothful human mass kept in a permanent state of backward subsistence by their reliance on the potato. The doctrinaire free traders wanted a wholesale shakeout of Irish agriculture: enclosure, modernisation, assisted passage schemes for tenants who were surplus to requirements, and so on. Because none of this was happening or likely to happen, Ireland was regarded by the free-trading Whigs as a chronic invalid.

In their eyes, the Famine was the inevitable consequence of this situation and an opportunity to remedy it. To many Whigs who were also devoutly evangelical, the Famine could be seen as the wrath of a righteous Protestant Providence.

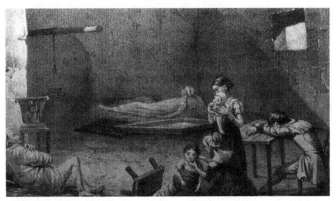

Interior of a Famine cottage

The government's strategic aim was to minimise its own direct involvement in Famine relief and make Ireland responsible for bearing the cost. The cost of local relief was to be borne by Irish landlords and the Poor Law system was expected to be the means whereby relief was given. This strategy was grounded in an assertion that a local crisis should be treated locally and should not become a burden on national finances. This assertion dovetailed neatly with the core value of free trade, that government interference in the economic mechanism was harmful and damaging in itself. There was no doubt that free trade had made Britain rich. But now it was making Ireland starve.

After the failure of 1846, people were reduced to eating seed potatoes. Ironically, the crop did not fail in 1847 but yields were low because so little had been sown. Black '47 entered the folk memory. People were not simply dying of starvation but also of the illnesses induced by starvation, especially typhus and relapsing fever. Vast hordes of sick and dying wandered the countryside, throwing themselves onto the workhouses established under the Poor Law system, which proved utterly inadequate to the task, a burden they were never intended to bear.

By now, press reports were appearing in London which gave a vivid picture of the distress. *The Times* sent the Dublin-born William Howard Russell – later to become the most famous war correspondent of the age – to the west of Ireland. His accounts of what he saw horrified him and his readers. *The Illustrated London News* carried images of starving people and Famine funerals in West Cork that are still shocking today. This resulted in a redoubling of private charitable relief and the opening of Famine funds. Private charities had been a significant force in the relief of distress since 1845, the Quakers in particular playing a heroic role.

The rise in mortality and distress in 1847 was overwhelming. The scaling down of public works left the poorest people destitute, so that many had no money to buy such grain as was available for purchase. The rudimentary public health system buckled under the strain. An economic recession in Britain itself meant business failures and unemployment in the industrial North of England, diverting some sympathy and relief away from Ireland and nearer to home.

Famine relief was primarily seen by the government as a local charge upon the Irish landlords and the poor law system. But the worse things got, the less local agencies could cope. The more landlords were stretched, the tougher the line they took with tenants unable to keep up their rental payments. Evictions increased, throwing ever more wretched, destitute and starving families on to the roads. Naturally, the main burden of this disaster fell upon the poor.

The quarter-acre clause
This process was accelerated in turn by a piece of legislation

known forever after as the Quarter-Acre Clause. The Poor Law Extension Act 1847 stated that 'occupiers of more than a quarter-acre of land are not to be deemed destitute, nor to be relieved out of the poor rates'. Thus starving peasants were faced with the need to surrender their tiny holdings in order to qualify for poor relief. Naturally, those who did so never recovered them. This piece of social engineering had the effect of consolidating the size of farms, a necessary and desirable reform in general terms but an extraordinary one to introduce in the circumstances. Its author was a Co. Galway landlord called Sir William Gregory. His wife Augusta Persse, many years his junior, would later achieve fame as Lady Gregory, *eminence grise* of the Irish literary revival. It is worth noting that a majority of O'Connell's MPs supported the Quarter-Acre Clause: utilitarian and free trade assumptions were not confined to British Whigs and Tories.

'The Day after the Ejectment', from the Illustrated London News 16 December 1848

Then the potato crop failed again in 1848. It was another catastrophic failure, as in 1846. The government made further poor relief dependent on the collection of arrears in the Poor Law rates. Nearly £1m. was duly collected but at the cost of growing agrarian unrest. Emigration beckoned for many. Landlords faced ruin. There were further minor failures of the potato crop up until 1852, although the worst of the devastation was over by 1849.

Catastrophic outcome

The 1851 census told the story simply. It recorded a population of just over 6.5 million people. The corresponding figure ten years earlier had been just under 8.2 million. The population of Ireland had been reduced by 20 per cent in a decade, over 1.5 million people. Of these, at least half died; the rest emigrated. Emigration became a way of life from then on, causing the population to decline to less than 4.4 million in 1911. In seventy years, the span of a single life, the population of Ireland was almost cut in half.

The Famine was a natural ecological disaster. The government's response made a disaster into a catastrophe. It applied an economic theory that may have made sense in the medium and long term but which had the immediate effect of exacerbating the distress. It held to its free trade beliefs with religious certainty – this in an age when religious belief informed every aspect of life in a manner no longer imaginable. Indeed, the contrast between Protestant material success and Catholic poverty had a melodramatic hold on many English minds. The Irish system of landholding and agriculture was indeed antique. It was overdue for reform, and the Famine was in that sense providential: the wrath of the Protestant god directed at the feckless and the lazy.

Almost a million people died in the process. Millions more emigrated, many taking with them a hatred of Britain for letting Ireland starve. Whether that was a fair or an unfair judgment, it was an understandable one. The last great subsistence crisis in Europe occurred in a part of the richest country in the world and its effects were made more severe than they otherwise might have been by the deliberate actions of that country's government.

The government was hypnotised by its ideology, sincerely so, but at the cost of its humanity.

The losers

There were winners and losers. The most obvious losers were the pre-Famine landless poor, who bore the heaviest casualties. Those who emigrated were in general marginally more prosperous. They had enough to get themselves to ports and to pay their passage. But they too lost the life they knew and were driven into exile. Many landlords were ruined. Two pieces of legislation called the Encumbered Estates Acts established procedures for the disposal of their estates. The new owners were usually less sentimental about traditional rural obligations than their predecessors had been.

In the long term, the union of Great Britain and Ireland was a loser. The Famine fatally weakened the moral legitimacy of British rule in Ireland. In the eyes of Irish nationalists, the constitutional assertion that Ireland was a fully integrated part of the metropolitan British state seemed more and more a fiction. Britain treated Ireland not as an equal part of the United Kingdom but as a troublesome colony.

The Famine radicalised nationalists. It coincided with Europe's 'year of revolutions', 1848. Just as the United Irishmen of the 1790s had been inspired by the French Revolution of 1789, so now the radical Young Irelanders – John Mitchel, William Smith O'Brien and others – were inspired by the Paris revolution that established the second republic in February 1848. They and others had formed themselves into the Irish Confederation in 1847 on the occasion of their final break with the repealers.

The movement was riddled with government informers and spies. Mitchel was arrested in May and convicted on a charge of treason-felony. He was transported for fourteen years, first to Bermuda and later to Van Diemen's Land (Tasmania). He escaped to America in 1853. There, he wrote *Jail Journal*, a bitterly anglophobe polemic that later became one of the sacred texts of Irish nationalism. He practised journalism and supported the Confederacy in the American civil war.

The remaining Confederation leaders were effectively harried out of Dublin by government pressure. They tried to raise troops for a possible autumn rising in Tipperary and Kilkenny. They held a meeting at Ballingarry, Co. Tipperary in July 1848 to discuss the way forward. A majority were for avoiding armed action, at least for the moment. A minority, led by O'Brien, was in favour. The issue was forced by a company of police which entered the village and took up a position in the house of Mrs McCormack, a widow. Some of O'Brien's more enthusiastic supporters attacked this position. Two insurgents were killed before the arrival of police reinforcements brought the affray to an end.

It was derided as the battle of the Widow McCormack's cabbage patch. But it was also remembered as the rising of 1848. However inflated that claim might have been, it was typical of the Young Ireland achievement. They were propagandists rather than men of action. Their legacy was the creation of a myth – or at least a part of a myth. While mainstream nationalism would eventually revive itself along a broadly O'Connellite model – constitutional politics and the support of the church – the memory of '48, like that of '98, was a reminder of other possibilities. Young Ireland, like the United Irishmen, became part of an internal opposition within Irish nationalism.

Departure of emigrants for the New World

The winners

The biggest winners of all in the fallout from the Famine were
the wealthier tenants, although this was by no means obvious at
the time. In the midst of the most appalling starvation and
destitution, they maintained their social position. Not all tenants
were poor. On the contrary, a comfortable tenant class and their
merchant cousins in the towns survived the Famine very well.
Once again, it is instructive to look at the foundation dates of
Catholic institutions in order to appreciate how economically
vigorous parts of the Catholic community remained in the
Famine years. Kilkenny's Cathedral of the Assumption was
begun in 1843; building continued until 1857. The parish
church of St Mary's in Clonmel, Co. Tipperary, is dated to
1837–50. St Aidan's Cathedral, Enniscorthy, Co. Wexford
(1843–8) was designed by Pugin, no less. He also designed the
Loreto convent in nearby Gorey.

All these examples are within the rich south-eastern quadrant,
where there were communities of Catholics wealthy enough to
endow and erect such impressive structures at a time when the
country was being engulfed in a demographic cataclysm. Nor
was the process any longer the exclusive preserve of the south-
east. The Catholic cathedral of St Patrick in Armagh was begun
in 1840; the Franciscan church in Galway dates from 1849; the
cathedral of SS Peter and Paul in Ennis, Co. Clare was
consecrated in 1843; that of St Mary's in Killarney (Pugin again)
in 1855 after thirteen years a-building.

While the real explosion in Catholic institutional building
does not happen until the second half of the nineteenth century,
what is significant is the degree to which the process is already
well established before and during the Famine. The people who
paid for all this – the Catholic provincial middle class – were the
group that profited most from the Famine.

The landlords and the whole Ascendancy world were
weakened. The rural poor were decimated. The social
engineering desired by the doctrinaire free traders was well under
way. Farm sizes grew. Sub-division of holdings was ended.
Enclosures proceeded and the system of communal agriculture
was finally abandoned in the west in favour of individual
holdings. Marriages were postponed until tenancies could be

inherited; younger children had to shift for themselves, often by emigrating. There was a deeply unsentimental social calculus in post-Famine Ireland. Among tenants, the watchword was 'never again', even though (or perhaps because) theirs was the class that emerged least scathed from the Famine. In a sense, the dirty work that enabled them to become the dominant social force in Ireland from the 1880s on had been done for them. And it could all be blamed on the British.

The Catholics who did well out of the Famine were the backbone of the land movement, of Parnell's electorate, of the Catholic laity and clergy, of the Gaelic Athletic Association, and of all subsequent nationalist agitation. It was their class that was celebrated and sentimentalised in Charles Kickham's *Knocknagow* and other novels of the virtuous rural life. It was their grandchildren, by and large, who inherited the independent Irish state in 1922.

6

A WORLD TRANSFORMED

The land question

The Famine changed Ireland irrevocably. It ushered in the age of
the farmer. Farmers became the key social group in post-Famine
Ireland. First as tenants, later as owner-occupiers, their material
interests became associated with those of the nation itself, a
situation that persisted until the economic changes of the 1960s
shifted the balance of power towards the urban middle class.

The key question in post-Famine Ireland was the land
question. In time, land and the national question became one.
In their own eyes, farmers were the real Irish nation. Agriculture
was simply the most important economic activity in the country
and much of the economic life of provincial Ireland depended
on the prosperity of farmers. In the towns, industries such as
brewing and distilling drew their raw materials from the
countryside.

As farm sizes increased, the basic shape of modern Irish
agriculture emerged. The key change was the shift from tillage to
pasture. A great deal of the tillage economy of the pre-Famine
period had been of the subsistence kind. That ended, as almost
all Irish agriculture went on to a commercial footing. Large
farms emerged, particularly in those flat eastern counties near
Dublin which were best suited for pasture. These holdings, often
referred to as 'ranches', were to be the source of ongoing
resentment from smallholders. In part, this was due to the no-
nonsense commercialism of the ranchers.

The ranchers were an interesting group. Many were Catholics
and nationalists, shopkeepers and other town dwellers who had
accumulated some capital and were in a position either to rent
or buy the large holdings for grazing. There was huge social
prestige attached to the ownership or control of land. The
ranchers were a new rural elite. Their position within the
broader nationalist consensus was anomalous. On the one hand,
they often provided the kind of social leadership and financial

support on which nationalist movements depended; on the other, they drew the fire of smallholders who asserted the superiority of tillage as the backbone of self-sufficient family farms. There was plenty of potential in all this for class war in the countryside – and it did break out from time to time, with cattle drives and other actions directed against the ranchers – but in general it was kept under control. Unity in the nationalist community overbore every other consideration, especially until the hated landlord system was dismantled in the early twentieth century.

Post-Famine Ireland was never classless. On the contrary, small social differences were often keenly felt in a manner typical of a provincial small-town and rural society. Both the rural and urban working classes – the landless agricultural labourers and the unskilled slum dwellers in the cities – were held in something between disdain and contempt by the prevailing *petit bourgeois* culture. Yet the imperative demands of national solidarity never permitted the development of fully blown class politics.

Turning towards Rome

In the aftermath of the Famine, nationalist Ireland was exhausted and demoralised. As politics atrophied, the Catholic Church filled the void. It was a church which was reinventing itself. The pre-Famine church had had a broadly Gallican thrust. This meant an emphasis on the autonomy of local bishops in matters of a civil and temporal nature. Spiritual matters were, of course, subject to full papal authority. Gallican ideas contrasted with ultramontanism, the view which stressed the central authority of Rome in all matters affecting Catholics.

In 1850, Paul Cullen was appointed archbishop of Armagh. Three years later, he was translated to Dublin and in 1866 he became the first Irish cardinal. He had been born in Co. Kildare in 1803 and ordained in Rome in 1829. In 1832, he was appointed rector of the Irish college in Rome. His entire formation as a cleric had therefore taken place in the shadow of the Vatican. He was recognised from the first as a person of exceptional ability: hard-working, rigorous, disciplined and intellectually accomplished. Cullen was an ultramontane by conviction and temperament alike.

St Macartan's Cathedral, Monaghan, assertive and dominating, reflecting the new centrality of the parish church

He was Rome's man in Ireland and he left an imprint on the Irish church that was not seriously shaken until the clerical sex scandals of the 1990s. The Catholic Church became the undisputed centre of moral authority in nationalist Ireland. No politician could ignore it.

Much has been made of the so-called devotional revolution in the Irish church. This was the process whereby Catholicism progressively abandoned traditional folk practices: patterns (gatherings at traditional shrines); wakes; stations (masses celebrated in private houses). The new emphasis was to be on uniform devotions conducted under formal clerical supervision in churches. Strict Sunday observance; regular attendance at confession and communion as decreed in canon law; the widespread introduction of continental devotions such as those to the Sacred Heart.

As with politics, the devotional revolution was most developed in the south-east of the island, less so (until Cullen's time) as one went north and west. The growth of church building in the second half of the century, and the assertive and dominating presence of so many fine churches, reflected the new centrality of the parish church in the lives of the faithful. In a sense, it represented the industrialisation of Irish Catholicism. The churches were like spiritual factories, where people now had to travel to worship at set times and in a disciplined manner ordained by their clerical overseers.

The Fenian Brotherhood

After the failure of 1848, the remains of the Young Irelanders scattered. Some, like John Mitchel, were transported. Others, like John Blake Dillon, escaped abroad before taking advantage of an amnesty in 1855 to return without ever again being a major force in politics. Charles Gavan Duffy was a Westminster MP for three years but gave it up in disgust and emigrated to Australia. He lived a long life, became prime minister of Victoria in 1871 and accepted a knighthood two years later before ending his days in retirement in the south of France.

No sub-set of Young Ireland was of greater importance for the future than the Fenians. The Fenian Brotherhood or Irish Republican Brotherhood (IRB) was founded jointly in Dublin and New York in 1858. The Dublin founder was James Stephens, an 1848 veteran who had fled to Paris where he had involved himself in various revolutionary secret societies. From them, he acquired the organisational principles he put in place in Ireland. The basic Fenian structure was this: a local leader, known as a centre, was chosen. Each centre chose nine captains who chose nine sergeants who chose nine men. Information was passed to each rank on a need-to-know basis only. Within a few years, Stephens had tramped the country and established a national network based on this structure.

The New York organisation was principally the work of John O'Mahony, another 1848 veteran. The introduction of Irish-America into the equation was a critical development: no subsequent nationalist movement has been indifferent to the enormous potential of the transatlantic diaspora.

The Fenians believed in the force of arms. They were a secret, militant, revolutionary society dedicated to the violent overthrow of British rule in Ireland and the establishment in its place of an independent Irish republic. They were uninterested in politics, with its trimming and prevarication. They borrowed their methods from the European left-wing secret society tradition. This brought them head to head with the Catholic Church.

The ultramontane Catholicism of Pope Pius IX was bitterly opposed to revolutionary secret societies. The church had been an uncompromising enemy of revolutionary France and a strong supporter of the reactionary regimes established after the final defeat of Napoleon. These regimes had been overturned in 1848 and Pius himself had had to flee from Rome for two years.

In these circumstances, it was inevitable that the church in Ireland would regard the Fenians as part of an international conspiracy against the legitimate order. Cullen was no friend of the British state but he was determined to ensure that Irish opposition to it was firmly under church control. He exercised effective control over loose alliances of Irish MPs at Westminster in the 1850s and 1860s, but these groups were never effective and never caught the public imagination.

The Fenians did. Stephens was a talented organiser and numbers swelled. In particular, Fenianism appealed to lower middle-class young men in the towns. This was a group significantly lower on the social scale than most of the Young Irelanders had been. In this sense, Fenianism played its own part in the democratisation of Irish nationalism.

Success inevitably meant police penetration, despite the cell structure. In 1865, Stephens and the leadership of the Fenians were arrested in a pre-emptive strike by the government. They had indeed been planning for a rising that year, hoping to exploit the services of Irish-American soldiers demobilised at the end of the American Civil War. The loss of momentum in 1865 was fatal and that generation of Fenians never recovered from it.

Stephens dithered on his release from prison. He sailed to New York and became fatally embroiled in the poisonous internal politics of the American Fenians.

Stephens was eventually deposed and a small group of American Fenians sailed to Ireland. In March 1867, they tripped off a feeble rising that was hardly more heroic as a feat of arms than 1848. But the aftermath was significant. First, the 1867 rising entered the apostolic succession of Irish rebellions. Second, Fenian prisoners became a focus of political agitation. Third, two of these prisoners were the subject of a rescue bid. A police van in Manchester containing the two Irish prisoners was attacked and the men released but a policeman was killed in the process. Three men, William Allen, Michael Larkin and William O'Brien, were hanged for this deed. These were the 'Manchester Martyrs' and their executions galvanised nationalist Ireland. The song 'God Save Ireland' was written in their memory and became the unofficial national anthem for the next two generations.

Ulster and the Industrial Revolution

There was another kind of revolution in Ireland at the mid-nineteenth century. The Industrial Revolution hardly affected the three southern provinces but it transformed Ulster. The term itself refers to a complex series of economic advances that began in Britain from the 1780s onwards and spread gradually and unevenly through Western Europe in the nineteenth century. The key developments were the harnessing of steam power, the accelerated development of coal and iron mining, the move from domestic piece work by individual craftsmen to factory production by armies of semi-skilled and unskilled workers. This development meant the growth of industrial cities and a surge of population from the countryside to the towns.

The Industrial Revolution had originated in Britain, where it was mainly focused in the midlands, north and west. Ireland, with its lack of iron and coal, seemed unpromising territory. But the exception proved to be in eastern Ulster, where the centralisation of the linen bleaching industry in Belfast marked the first stage in the industrialisation of the province and the beginning of Belfast's phenomenal expansion in Victorian times.

Its population in 1808 was about 25,000; in 1901, it was almost 350,000.

In 1828, the York Street linen mill was established. An enormous premises by the industrial standards of the times, it became the focus of Belfast's pre-eminence as a centre of the international linen trade. By 1850, there were sixty-two such mills in Belfast alone. The need to import coal and flax – because the industry had expanded beyond the ability of local resources to supply the mills – meant the development of Belfast port. From this, there grew the shipbuilding industry which was the city's pride in the late Victorian and Edwardian eras.

In 1858 Edward Harland bought a small shipyard in Belfast Lough. Three years later, he went into partnership with Gustav Wilhelm Wolff. Harland & Wolff was to become one of the giants of British shipbuilding: it built the most famous ship ever to sail and sink, the *Titanic*, in 1912. A smaller yard, that of Workman Clark ('the wee yard'), was established on the Lagan in 1880 where it flourished until the Great War before finally closing in 1935.

It was not just linen and ships. The Belfast region produced other textiles, tobacco products, engineering and other commodities typical of the new industrial age. In effect, Ulster became part of the economy of north-west Britain. Its economic fortunes could hardly have made a greater contrast with the agricultural provinces to the south, reeling from the effects of the Famine. The leaders of industry in Ulster were almost all Protestants: their identification with their co-religionists in Britain was augmented by common economic and material interests. Ulster was growing ever more apart from the three southern provinces.

Behind the impressive modernity of industrial Ulster, however, there loomed the long shadow of sectarian hatred. Industrial-isation meant migration from country to town and the migrants brought their ancient enmities with them. As early as 1850, Belfast in particular was a city segregated by confessional allegiance, especially in working-class areas. There were serious inter-communal riots in 1857, 1864, 1872 and 1886, a tradition that deepened in the twentieth century and is still virulently present in the city today.

The nineteenth century was an age of faith. Religion was central to life and to people's belief systems in a way that is almost beyond the understanding of even the most devout modern believer. Religious differences were sharply felt, doctrinal and theological rivalries keenly contested. This was true of Europe in general. In Ireland, such differences were sharpened by the overlay of inherited ethnic and class polarities. But Ulster was a special case. Nowhere else in Ireland was the balance of populations so volatile and unstable or the burden of the past so oppressive. Ulster was not only running on a course different to that of the other three provinces. It was doing so in the face of internal divisions that had their roots in the seventeenth century and that were being renewed and strengthened in every generation.

7

THE NATION *IN VITRO*

Gladstone: addressing the grievances

A new prime minister, William Ewart Gladstone, took office in 1868. One of the most remarkable of all the Victorians, he was the first British statesman to attempt to wrestle honestly with the challenge of Irish nationalism. Shaken by the Fenian campaign – not just the attempted rising in Ireland but also by a huge bomb in London that killed seventeen people – he determined to find solutions for genuine grievances.

Gladstone's first legislative measure was the disestablishment of the Church of Ireland. Although the largest Protestant denomination in the country, it still accounted for barely 12 per cent of the total population. It had been the established church since Henry VIII's break with Rome in the 1530s and its position as the official state church had been confirmed by the Act of Union, which united it to the Church of England. Disestablishment therefore unravelled a key provision of the union settlement. The logic of this was not lost on unionists, for if one provision could be set aside what was to stop the whole thing being subverted?

Gladstone next turned to tackle an issue that went to the very heart of Irish discontent: land. There were to be eighteen Irish land acts passed between 1870 and 1903, all intended to equalise the relationship between landlord and tenant by positive discrimination in favour of the latter. Gladstone's act of 1870 was the start of this process. It gave legal force to certain customary practices, in particular a departing tenant's right to be compensated for improvements made by him and the right to sell his interest to the highest bidder subject to the landlord's approval of the purchaser. These customary rights, which had been generally confined to Ulster, were now extended to the whole country by force of law.

William Gladstone became Prime Minister in 1868

Call for home rule

On 1 September 1870 the Home Government Association was launched in Dublin by Isaac Butt, a barrister and former MP. Its basic demand was for some form of devolved autonomy for Ireland or, in the brilliantly vague term in which it couched the demand, home rule.

The term was deliberately elastic. In the early days, in Butt's formulation, it amounted to a call for devolved domestic parliaments for Ireland, Scotland and England (but not for Wales). Westminster would remain sovereign and would deal with foreign and imperial matters.

Part of home rule's early appeal lay with some members of the Church of Ireland who felt betrayed by disestablishment and who thought that a Dublin parliament could be a better safeguard for Protestant interests. Butt himself was a Protestant.

As the 1870s wore on, the home rule movement took on a more overtly nationalist hue. Constitutional nationalists and ex-Fenians were drawn to it; it also attracted the support of parish clergy, although not yet of the hierarchy. In the 1874 general election that ousted Gladstone and installed Disraeli, candidates pledged to home rule won 59 seats. But they did not constitute a party in any modern sense. Butt was a gentlemanly but ineffective leader; he lost the support of many of his original Protestant adherents without gaining the confidence of the Catholic hierarchy; and the Fenian and neo-Fenian element among his MPs were effectively out of his control. From 1876 on, they began disruptive filibustering tactics in Westminster.

This unseemly challenge to the decorum of the house eventually forced a change in its rule with the introduction of the 'guillotine' to foreclose debates. It also threw up an alternative to Butt. His name was Charles Stewart Parnell. He was from an old Co. Wicklow landed family and was MP for Co. Meath since 1875. He ousted Butt as party leader in 1880.

The previous year, he had acquired an even more important position when he became president of the Land League. This organisation had been founded in October 1879 mainly due to the energy and drive of Michael Davitt, the son of an evicted tenant farmer from Co. Mayo. An ex-Fenian with a conviction for gun-running, Davitt was dedicated to the wholesale overthrow of the landlord system.

The founding of the Land League coincided with an agricultural depression and a consequent reduction in agricultural earnings. The threat of eviction loomed for tenants unable to pay their rent. Memories of the Famine only a generation old stiffened the determination to resist. Irish-American money provided the means to organise. A loose administrative structure meant that the best organised and most ruthless could dominate the organisation, and that meant Fenians and other advanced nationalists. The demand was simple: peasant proprietorship.

Parnell therefore found himself at the head of an organisation whose essential demand was revolutionary. In the summer of 1879, he already had good contacts with Fenians on both sides of the Atlantic and had their confidence. In 1879, a deal was agreed between the Supreme Council of the IRB – the Irish Republican Brotherhood, the formal name for the Fenians – and Parnell's supporters in the home rule party. This was the so-called New Departure.

The land war

The New Departure meant the organisational and financial support of Fenianism for parliamentary action in return for the prosecution of new policies. First, there was to be a totally independent Irish party at Westminster without ties to any national British party and dedicated to Irish self-government. Butt's federal idea was to be scrapped. Second, the land agitation was to be brought to parliament in the form of a demand for legislation to create a peasant proprietorship.

An evicted tenant and his family

By the autumn of 1880, the land war was in full swing. Across the country – except, significantly, in most of Ulster – agrarian protesters who previously had merely sought rent abatements in view of the recession were now demanding the abolition of the entire landlord system. Evictions were resisted by violence; where they occurred, revenge was taken on landlords either by attacks on themselves or their livestock; murders, burnings and boycotting increased.

The land war escalated into a wholesale attack on the landlords not just for what they were but for what they represented: the British connection. They were portrayed as a British garrison holding Ireland for the crown against the will of the people. The stakes were raised to the point where the social authority of the ascendancy was fatally wounded. The absolute communal solidarity of the tenants, under the leadership of the Land League, was now the key agent of social control. To take up a farm from which another had been evicted was to guarantee being boycotted (the word originated in the land war: the eponym was Capt Charles Boycott, a land agent in Co. Mayo). Land League courts effectively supplanted crown courts in many parts of rural Ireland.

Gladstone returned to power in 1880 and embarked on a twin policy of coercion and conciliation. The use of special police powers to curb the excesses of the Land League was combined with a substantial concession to them. Gladstone's second Land Act – that of 1881 – conceded the demands known as the 'Three Fs': the right of free sale by an outgoing tenant; fixity of tenure to replace ordinary tenancies; and a fixed rent to be determined by land courts. Parnell at first opposed the act on the grounds that it was not radical enough. The government lodged him in Kilmainham prison in Dublin whereupon rural crime escalated out of control. He was released as part of the 'Kilmainham Treaty', whereby he undertook to accept the act – with some cosmetic improvements – in return for using his influence to quell the agitation. The Kilmainham Treaty was an acknowledgement by the government that Parnell was, in the famous phrase, the uncrowned king of Ireland.

Even the hideous Phoenix Park murders of May 1882, less than a month after the Kilmainham Treaty, did not shake the new Gladstone-Parnell alliance. A group called the Invincibles – Fenian ultras – set upon Lord Frederick Cavendish, the new chief secretary of Ireland, and Thomas Burke, the under-secretary, as they were walking in the Phoenix Park in Dublin. Using surgical knives, they killed them both. Public opinion on both sides of the water was horrified. Parnell, fearing that his whole strategy was compromised, offered his resignation to Gladstone (not to his own party). Gladstone declined it.

The government outlawed the Land League, but the movement was already split between those who were happy with the new act and the radicals. Besides, Parnell was quite happy to see the end of the League, for in his eyes it had served its purpose. He himself, as might be expected of a landlord, was not an agrarian radical. He had ridden the tiger to a position of influence such as no one had had in Ireland since O'Connell. Its work was done and he was content to dispense with it.

Besides, the Irish-American Fenian ultras spent much of the 1880s involved in a sporadic campaign of dynamite bombing in England. A 'skirmishing fund' was established to finance this activity, which in concept and method anticipated the IRA campaigns of a century later. The Tower of London, underground stations, Scotland Yard and even the chamber of the House of Commons itself were all targeted before the campaign was suppressed by the police in 1887. Among the many Fenians sentenced for their parts in this campaign was Thomas J. Clarke, destined to be the first signatory of the proclamation of the republic in 1916. The dynamite campaign was yet another reason for Parnell to distance himself from Fenian extremists while keeping mainstream Fenians safely on board the party ship.

He turned to the cause that really held his interest: home rule.

Parnell, the Chief

In October 1882, the organisation that succeeded the Land League was formed. Called the National League, it was firmly under Parnell's control; its purpose was to harness the mass support that had secured the 1881 Land Act for home rule and to act as a constituency organisation for the Nationalist party, as we may now begin to call the home rule MPs.

The National League controlled the constituencies and the candidates chosen. Each candidate had to pledge to support and vote with the Nationalist party at Westminster, failing which he undertook to resign. Everything was centralised and local particularism – never very subterranean in Ireland – was suppressed. At the apex of the entire structure was Parnell, the Chief. This structure was borrowed from Irish-American municipal politics, where ruthless discipline had delivered big-city administrations into Irish hands. The American Fenians who had insisted on an independent, pledge-bound party at Westminster as one of the terms of the New Departure knew what they were at. Tammany Hall came to the banks of the Thames.

The other key factor in the rise of the Nationalist party was its alliance with the Catholic church. This is one of those phenomena that seem perfectly natural in hindsight, but which were much more problematic in practice. Parnell was a Protestant; he had close associations – to put it no stronger – with the Fenians; and he had directed and exploited the Land League agitation, of which the church was deeply suspicious because of its subversion of the civic order.

On the other hand, it was clear that the Nationalists were an overwhelmingly Catholic party. Even in Butt's day a significant number of them had been loud champions of Catholic causes, most crucially that of denominational education. It was also clear that the National League was vastly more disciplined than the Land League had been. Dr Thomas Croke, the nationalist archbishop of Cashel, was an early supporter of Parnell. Others followed. The crucial alliance was forged in 1884, when the hierarchy agreed to throw the moral and organisational weight of the church behind the party; in return the party undertook to promote Catholic educational concerns in parliament.

Denominational education was a central concern of the church throughout the nineteenth century. The bishops founded a Catholic University in Dublin in 1854, with no less a person than Cardinal Newman as its first rector. It was the forerunner of UCD, now the country's biggest university. The hierarchy was determined to resist state interference in Catholic education at every level. The agreement between Parnell and the bishops meant that the party would act as a parliamentary watchdog in this matter.

Archibishop Thomas Croke of Cashel

In the general election of 1885, the Nationalists won 86 seats and found themselves holding the balance of power in the House of Commons. After a brief tactical flirtation with the Conservatives, Parnell renewed the Liberal alliance. It was a telling moment. Parnell had always insisted on the absolute independence of the party. Now political realities were dictating otherwise. It was the Liberals or nothing. The price he extracted was the introduction of the first Irish Home Bill by Gladstone in 1886. It split the Liberal party and was defeated. The Liberals fell from power, not to return – except for a brief interlude in the early 1890s – for twenty years.

None the less, it had been a stunning achievement. A bill to create an Irish parliament to deal with domestic affairs had been sponsored on the floor of the House of Commons by the prime minister. Its defeat was less significant than the fact that it had happened at all. What had been unthinkable ten years earlier was now a central fact of political life. Like all great politicians, Parnell made the weather. The Irish Question was on the British agenda. It would remain there in one form or another until the 'solution' of 1920-22. Its aftershocks are there to the present day.

In defence of the union

Of the 86 seats secured by the Nationalists in the 1885 election, 17 were in Ulster. This represented a simple majority of the province's 33 seats. The other 16 were all Conservatives. Ulster Liberalism was destroyed at the polls. Tenants on both sides of the sectarian divide who had previously voted Liberal now chose the Conservatives (if Protestant) to defend the union or Nationalists (if Catholic) to subvert it. Politics in the province took on the reductive form it has had ever since: for or against the union.

Combined with Gladstone's conversion to home rule, this was the moment of truth for Ulster Protestants. They mobilised a pan-Protestant movement in defence of the union. They feared that what they regarded as the backward, agricultural, Catholic south would overwhelm the progressive, industrial, Protestant north. Confessional and material self-interest dovetailed neatly.

Ulster Conservatives now moved closer to the Orange Order, with its tradition of cross-class popular mobilisation. Borrowing freely from nationalist techniques, they organised a series of mass meetings across the province culminating in a mass rally in the Ulster Hall in Belfast on 22 February 1886. The principal speaker was Lord Randolph Churchill, the dazzlingly unstable younger son of the Duke of Marlborough and father of Winston. Churchill's formula, 'Ulster will fight, and Ulster will be right', became a rallying cry for Ulster Protestants.

The defeat of the Home Rule Bill two months later seemed like a deliverance. The return of the Conservatives under Lord Salisbury removed the immediate danger but the crisis had changed the political landscape in Ulster forever.

The tensions surrounding the home rule crisis tripped off the worst sectarian rioting that Belfast had yet seen. From June to September, the riots went on sporadically, leaving an official death count of 31, although unofficial estimates suggested nearer 50. Belfast, more than ever before, was a city divided absolutely along sectarian lines. In this, it reflected the wider Ulster reality which was determined by the delicate confessional demography of the province.

The fall of Parnell

To Parnell and the Nationalists, the defeat of the Home Rule bill seemed just a temporary setback. The immense prestige of Gladstone lay behind the cause; Parnell's reputation had never stood higher; it seemed only a matter of time before the natural pendulum of British politics would restore the Liberals to power and home rule to the political agenda.

In 1889 *The Times* falsely accused Parnell of conspiring with the Invincibles in the Phoenix Park Murders of 1882 and of approving the deaths of Cavendish and Burke. The whole thing was based on the forgeries of one Richard Pigott. A commission of inquiry exposed the fraud, leaving Parnell's public position stronger than ever. On his return to the Commons, he got a standing ovation. He was just 43 years of age, at the height of his powers, adored in nationalist Ireland, respected and feared at Westminster, the undisputed leader of a nation-in-waiting. It was this that made his fall so shocking.

For many years, Parnell had lived with Katharine O'Shea, the estranged wife of Capt William O'Shea MP. O'Shea had squandered an inheritance and proved an incompetent businessman before entering politics in 1880. He lost his seat in 1885. He knew of the affair between Parnell and his wife and tolerated it. He could not afford to sue for divorce, since he was dependent for financial support on an elderly aunt of Katherine's who would have been scandalised by such a course. She eventually died, at which point Willie O'Shea's inhibitions deserted him. He sued for divorce, citing his wife's adultery and naming Parnell as co-respondent.

Amazingly, nationalist solidarity held. The Catholic bishops clearly disapproved of the behaviour of the Protestant adulterer but stayed their hand. The parliamentary party prepared to re-elect Parnell as leader. It was at this point that elements in the Liberal party withdrew their support for Parnell. The nonconformist conscience was being exercised.

There was a strong element of Christian moral earnestness in some Liberals' support for home rule: Gladstone himself was animated by it. Now these Liberals were telling Gladstone that Parnell's continued leadership of the Nationalist party would subvert the Liberal alliance. He was in their eyes a morally unfit

Charles Stewart Parnell

person. Gladstone was faced with either sacrificing Parnell or losing the leadership of Liberalism. He presented the Nationalists with a hideous dilemma. They could have Parnell or the Liberal alliance but not both.

The party split on 15 December 1890. The majority chose the Liberals. Parnell attempted to reconstruct his political fortunes in a series of three bitterly fought by-election campaigns in Ireland over the following year, all of which he lost. The church, determined not to be out-moralised by a crowd of English Protestants, turned against him. The split was a savage business, with passions inflamed beyond reason on both sides. It darkened Irish nationalist life for a generation.

Parnell's frenzied by-election campaigns killed him. Never robust, he was drenched to the skin while addressing a meeting in Creggs, Co. Roscommon and caught a chill which developed into pneumonia. He dragged himself back to Brighton, where he lived with Katharine, and died there on 6 October 1891. His remains were returned to Dublin where his funeral attracted over 100,000 mourners. He is buried in the most impressive grave in Ireland, in Glasnevin cemetery under a single boulder of Wicklow granite bearing the simple legend PARNELL.

8

INTERREGNUM

Settling the land question

With the death of Parnell and the party split between the anti-Parnellite majority and the Parnellite minority, the 1890s was a wretched decade for the politics of Irish nationalism. The Nationalists eventually reunited in 1900 under the leadership of John Redmond, who had headed the Parnellite faction. The assumption of the leadership by someone from the smaller group was a conscious attempt to bind up wounds. But while the party gradually recovered its sense of purpose, it never regained the iron unity and discipline of Parnell's day.

In the meantime, the Conservative governments of Lord Salisbury resumed their policy of 'killing home rule with kindness'. This meant social and economic reforms and initiatives designed to prove that good government was better than self-government. The policy had first been articulated under a previous Tory government in the late 1880s and early 1890s. The then chief secretary, Arthur Balfour, had established the Congested Districts Board in 1891 to assist in development schemes for the poorer parts of the country – mainly along the Atlantic seaboard. The initiatives included infrastructural developments: many of the country's quaint narrow-gauge railways were financed by the board. Harbours were constructed. Cottage crafts and education in modern agricultural methods were encouraged.

The Local Government Act of 1898 modernised an antique system, sweeping away grand juries and poor law boards and establishing democratically elected county councils and urban councils. This had the important effect of making numbers count at local level, replacing unionists with nationalists in most cases. Many stalwarts of the Irish revolution first cut their political teeth in these local assemblies.

The most momentous piece of legislation came in 1903, when the chief secretary, George Wyndham, introduced the Land Act that has ever since borne his name. The Conservatives had long been of the view that a move to tenant purchase was the solution to the land question, which had flared up intermittently ever since the suppression of the Land League.

The 1903 Act provided government funds to buy out the Irish landlords and transfer the land to the former tenants who now became independent proprietors. Thus the independent family farm came to pass. The act resulted from a conference at which all interests had been represented, so it was a consensual piece of legislation. This was a remarkable achievement, considering the mayhem in the countryside a mere twenty years earlier. The purchasers were given long-term loans by the government. The repayments, over thirty-five years, generally annualised at a lower figure than the old rents. From the landlords' point of view, payments were in cash rather than bonds and the government offered a 12 per cent premium for estates that were sold in their entirety.

No piece of legislation in any parliament has had such a transforming effect on the country. It was the moment of triumph for the former tenants, who were now not just established as proprietors but soon would be the most significant social group in the country. Now they were an interest, no longer a cause: one of the ironies of their triumph is that the Nationalist party no longer had its core issue to rally and unite it. The land question was effectively settled.

The Gaelic League

In 1893, the Gaelic League was formed. The founder was Eoin Mac Néill, an historian of early and medieval Ireland. The first president was Douglas Hyde, the son of a Church of Ireland rector from Co. Roscommon. A scholar and linguist, he had delivered a lecture in 1892 under the title 'The Necessity for De-anglicising the Irish People', in which he called for an arrest in the decline of the Irish language and deplored the advance of what he regarded as a vulgar, English commercial culture.

The new organisation established itself quickly. It had as its aim the revival of Irish as the common vernacular. It conducted language classes. It published stories, plays and a newspaper, *An Claidheamh Soluis* (The Sword of Light). It opposed a campaign led by Mahaffy, the Provost of Trinity College Dublin, to have the language removed from the Intermediate school syllabus. It established language teacher training colleges. By 1908, there were 600 branches of the League around the country.

The Gaelic League successfully revived the Young Irelanders' idea that cultural and linguistic autonomy was a good thing, and was part of a greater national revival. Hyde naïvely thought that the language was a non-political issue on which people of all religious and social backgrounds could meet without rancour. The League was indeed non-political for the first twenty-two years of its life. But its implied purpose was clear: the re-Gaelicisation of Ireland. In some ways, it was a very Victorian phenomenon, appealing to the same kind of medieval nostalgia that animated the pre-Raphaelites and the arts and crafts movement in England.

The literary revival

By injecting a strong cultural element into the national mix, the Gaelic League was part of a larger movement that developed from the 1890s onwards. What is commonly called the Irish literary revival was the work of a remarkable generation of writers and intellectuals. It is often represented as a reaction to the sordid politics of the Parnell split and a search for a more honourable and positive means of expressing national sentiment. It drew inspiration from the Young Ireland poets associated with *The Nation* as well as from the work of antiquarians and Celtic scholars in Ireland and on the continent. Like all such movements, it required a central figure and found it in the poet W.B. Yeats.

Yeats was not simply a man of genius but also a very considerable man of action. He had started publishing in the late 1880s and continued in the following decade. His influential *Celtic Twilight* collection appeared in 1893 and gave the entire movement a name that stuck. Yeats was fascinated by mysticism and eastern religion and managed to translate both to a Celtic locale. He shared this enthusiasm with many leading figures in the movement, most notably the remarkable George Russell (AE), and in temper the literary movement was romantic and anti-utilitarian.

William Butler Yeats

It was also, to a remarkable degree for a movement of its kind, Protestant. Yeats, Russell and Lady Gregory, the patron and *eminence grise* of the movement, were all Protestants. So were Synge and O'Casey, its two great dramatists, and many of its minor figures. It has been speculated that they represented an enlightened Protestant vanguard, aware that the game was up for the old order with the disestablishment of the Church of Ireland and the end of the estate system, and anxious to find a role and make a stamp on the new Ireland.

The clash of politics and culture
The Gaelic League and the literary revival overlapped in places and shared a common sensibility. Both were anti-utilitarian and romantic. This brought both movements, but especially the literary revival, onto a collision course with the very utilitarian Catholic middle class. This group was the backbone of actual, living nationalist society. It had little interest in mystic

speculation, although its national pride was flattered by the dramatic representation of Irish heroic myths. Yeats's play, *Cathleen Ni Houlihan*, first given in Dublin in 1902, was a thinly disguised call to arms against England and famously gave the poet qualms of conscience in later years.

Yeats was many things, including a Fenian sympathiser (perhaps even an actual Fenian for a while), but was consistent in his distaste for the middle class. He disdained the very people who were inheriting the new nationalist world. The farmers, shopkeepers, clerks and others of this sort who had been the backbone of Parnell's party had other voices to articulate their concerns and prejudices, not least D.P. Moran, a journalist with a supreme talent for abuse. His journal, *The Leader*, founded in 1900, was a scabrously entertaining cocktail of lower-middle class nationalist prejudice against Protestants, intellectuals, the English, the rich, nationalists like Arthur Griffith of whom Moran did not approve, and anything and anyone that caught the editor's ire. Moran was a bottomless pit of acid.

Yeats's world and Moran's collided in 1907 when Synge's *Playboy of the Western World* opened at the Abbey. Yeats and Lady Gregory had founded the theatre three years earlier: it was one of the monumental achievements of the revival. Patriotic plays were one thing. The gritty realism of Synge was another. The *Playboy* is set in Co. Mayo and the peasant cast is presented, in part at least, as ignorant, credulous and superstitious. This was deeply offensive to a nationalist audience, which saw only stage-Irish caricature. They also shared the prissy puritanism of the age, so when a reference was made to a 'shift' – a lady's undergarment or slip – it was the trigger for an already shocked and tense audience to riot.

The *Playboy* riot was not simply a contest between art and philistinism, although this was naturally the myth that Yeats made of it. It was a collision of different mental worlds. Ironically, both were attempting a definition of Irishness and its place in the world that was transforming. For the utilitarian middle class, virtue meant material progress, piety, respectability and movement towards home rule. Indeed, if you subtract the political element, the nationalist middle class had aspirations very similar to their counterparts in the rest of the United

Kingdom. After the trauma of the Famine, less than a lifetime before, the advance in material fortunes was a source of pride. Synge's peasants seemed like some sort of pre-Famine horror, drawn by a condescending Protestant in a theatre run by the widow of Sir William Gregory – he of the Famine quarter-acre clause.

For Yeats and Synge, the autonomy of great art and its fidelity to reality was the supreme virtue. Part of the problem for the audience was precisely that Synge was not drawing stage-Irish characters: they were all too real. Synge had spent many nights in western cottages, listening and noting the vocabulary, syntax and utterances of western peasants. It was his fidelity in reproducing their speech – these people who were now a social embarrassment to the new bourgeoisie – that was troubling. Set in the context of a powerful psychological drama, a truly stirring work of art, the tension proved too great.

That tension was caused by a gap between politics and culture in nationalist Ireland that nothing could bridge in the early twentieth century. Nationalist politics had focused on the material, most obviously on the land question. Its organisational methods were borrowed from Tammany Hall and were not for the squeamish. It was hand in glove with the Catholic clergy. It was careful and calculating. The cultural revival occurred after O'Connell and Parnell had set the material template for nationalism. It attempted to overlay a cultural template and to furnish nationalism with myths and symbols. In this, it had considerable success but its sensibility was always at an oblique angle to the utilitarianism of the political and social mainstream. Unlike many other European nationalisms, where the culture came first and the politics second, in Ireland it was the other way round. In the end, as Yeats would discover, the politics would crush the culture, demanding of it a role subservient to the wishes and prejudices of the new dominant class. Nationalism cannibalised the cultural revival for those titbits it could digest. It rejected the rest.

The Gaelic Athletic Association
If the Gaelic League attempted to stay non-political, the other key cultural organisation of the period from the Parnell split to

the Easter Rising had no such inhibitions. On the contrary, the Gaelic Athletic Association (GAA) was a Fenian vehicle from the start. It has also been the most successful popular association in modern Irish history.

It was founded in Thurles, Co. Tipperary in 1884. Its purpose was to preserve and promote the ancient game of hurling. In addition, it developed a code of football which went on to become the most popular spectator sport in twentieth-century Ireland. For the Fenians, it offered a perfect recruiting vehicle and its politics reflected Fenian radicalism right from the beginning. It was aggressively Parnellite at the time of the split and thereafter was to be found on the left of the nationalist movement on every occasion. It was republican in politics; hugely supportive of the Irish language and of Gaelic culture in general; tacitly Catholic, although not clerical, in its assumptions; and ferociously opposed to the symbols of British rule, not least the police. It imposed a ban on its members playing 'foreign games' – defined as soccer, rugby, hockey and cricket – which lasted until 1971.

In part, it was a reaction against the exclusiveness of other sports. Rugby was focused on elite private schools; cricket had a long association with both army and ascendancy; athletics was administered by a Trinity College elite which discouraged, to put it no more strongly, the participation of the wrong sort of chaps. The GAA was perfect for the people whose faces did not fit. To be fair, this point can easily be exaggerated: there is much local evidence from the late 1880s, when things were still fluid, that GAA clubs were founded by athletes who cheerfully played cricket and association football (soccer). The exclusiveness was not all one way: the ban on foreign games was also a form of exclusion, a kind of recreational tariff wall willed by the Fenian element in the GAA for political-cultural reasons.

At any rate, the GAA became *the* great popular mobilising force in Irish recreational life. And it did so in a context that applauded exclusion, that insisted on the separateness of Gaelic games and the social life that revolved around them. Games were played on Sundays, the only free day in the working week, which guaranteed that sabbatarian Protestants were unlikely to participate. The GAA soon spread to every Catholic parish in the country, with a local club often named for a saint or a patriot: thus Naomh (Saint) this-or-that, plus various Emmets, Tones, Sarsfields and so on. There were few named for O'Connell, whose aversion to violence made him *persona non grata* in Fenian eyes. This was ironic, given that its organisational structure so clearly mirrored O'Connell's own.

The GAA, the most Fenian and anglophobe of all nationalist organisations, was also a very modern phenomenon. The codification of sports – a mid-Victorian phenomenon – means the establishment of uniform rules for a game from a multitude of regional variants. Their antecedents of soccer and rugby were local rough-and-tumbles with local rules. Cricket had a number of regional antecedents like stoolball (which could have as easily evolved into baseball as into cricket). Eventually, cricket was codified on the rules of the game as played in Kent, Surrey and Hampshire. The West Country and Yorkshire variations now had to accommodate themselves to the new national standard. In baseball, the New York game displaced rival versions such as town ball and the so-called Massachusetts game. All this was a product of the railway revolution, which made national championships possible for the first time, and therefore led to a requirement for a uniform set of rules. The codification of hurling followed a path. The game had been particularly popular in three areas in pre-Famine times: in south Leinster and east Munster; on either side of the middle reaches of the Shannon, where east Galway looks across to south Offaly and north-west Tipperary; and in the Glens of Antrim. The Famine dealt what was nearly a death blow to the game in the first two areas: · indeed, cricket waxed strong in these areas in the post-Famine years. It was the need to revive hurling that inspired the founders of the association. And revive it they did. But in codifying the game they faced a problem. The game played in the Glens of Antrim was significantly different to the southern game. Unsurprisingly, given the ancient association between Antrim and the west of Scotland (the Mull of Kintyre is plainly visible from the Antrim coast on a fine day), the game played there was closer to Scottish shinty. The two games, while clearly related, have very obvious differences. Modern hurling was codified along the lines of the South Leinster game. Antrim had to adjust accordingly if it was to participate at national level. This interesting little exercise in internal imperialism was typical of how most sports were codified. The GAA may have been exclusive and different, but it obeyed the logic of all national sporting associations engaged in similar exercises.

Hurling, a century after the GAA was founded

9

THE IRISH REVOLUTION

~~~

Redmond's hour

The political flux following the Parnell split produced a situation in which radical and maverick groups flourished. They created a focus for their energies in 1905 with the founding of Sinn Féin. Its leading figure, Arthur Griffith, was not himself a republican. He espoused a dual monarchy along the line of the Austro-Hungarian settlement of 1867. Sinn Féin attracted support from all radical quarters and was a kind of internal opposition within the bigger nationalist tent.

It is important not to exaggerate the importance of the early Sinn Féin. It was simply the most prominent of a number of radical nationalist groups, both in the political and cultural spheres. The later centrality of Sinn Féin should not blind us to its marginality in the first decade of the twentieth century. Especially after the return of the Liberals to power in Westminster in 1905, the Nationalist party's fortunes began to improve although in retrospect a key difference emerges between Parnell's party and Redmond's. Parnell embraced the Fenians and contained them within the party structure. Redmond never had them securely on board. Until 1912 or so, this did not seem to matter. After 1916, it was fatal to Redmond's fortunes.

The 1910 election produced a hung parliament and, sure enough, the Liberal leader Asquith could only form a government with Redmond's support. Home rule was back on the agenda. In April 1912, the third Home Rule bill was introduced in the House of Commons. After ferocious Conservative opposition, it was not carried until January 1913. Predictably, it was then defeated in the Lords. However, the Parliament Act of 1911 had removed the Lords' veto, replacing it with a delaying power of two years. This meant that home rule would become a reality in 1914. The 1912 bill was Redmond's apotheosis. Parnell's dream, it seemed, was about to come true. Except, of course, that it never did.

Ulster opposition to home rule

In March 1905, the Ulster Unionist Council was formed in Belfast. Northern unionists had been alarmed at the conciliatory manner of their southern counterparts during the negotiations that preceded the Land Act of 1903. The differences between southern and northern unionism were clear. In the south, the remnants of the old ascendancy were reduced in fortune, land and prestige. In the north, a self-confident commercial aristocracy had been created by the industrial revolution.

The formation of the UUC announced the end of intra-Protestant rivalry and the creation of a communal solidarity that reflected that on the nationalist, Catholic side. Given the fractious nature of Protestantism, with its emphasis on individual conscience and judgment, this was a more difficult task than it seemed. Indeed, the kind of organisational unity represented by the UUC was easiest to sustain in times of crisis. When the crisis passed or abated, the underlying tensions resurfaced.

The real crisis for Ulster unionism came with the introduction of the third Home Rule bill. With the power of the Lords now emasculated, it meant that victory in the Commons would be enough to force the measure through. But the bill was anathema to all unionists. They had four advantages in their opposition to home rule: first, they were passionate about it and prepared to go to any extreme to win; second, they had a local majority in their Ulster heartland; third, they had the enthusiastic support of the Conservative party in Britain; finally, they had two leaders of real ability.

Edward Carson became leader of the UUC in 1910. Born in Dublin, he was a barrister in London, where his most celebrated performance had been in the destruction of Oscar Wilde at his trial in 1895. Carson was a commanding and rather mercurial figure, who brought immense prestige and good Conservative connections to the Ulster cause. In fact, the cause for him was that of Irish unionism *tout court*, although the practical focus was on Ulster. He was in the O'Connell-Parnell mould of Irish leader, urging radicalism and mass mobilisation to squeeze concessions from London. For that, he needed a mass movement. James Craig, a hatchet-faced millionaire typical of the new money plutocracy, gave it to him.

A series of meetings and rallies and an effective publicity campaign ensured that public opinion in Protestant Ulster was thoroughly mobilised. The campaign culminated in Ulster Day, 28 September 1912, with the signing of Ulster's Solemn League and Covenant by almost a quarter of a million men. This document or pledge was a conscious echo of the Solemn League and Covenant of 1643, in which Scots Presbyterians and English parliamentarians had united against the government of King Charles I. The historical parallel of united opposition to overweening authority was irresistible. The whole exercise was a brilliant *coup de théâtre*.

It became clear to the government that some concession would have to be made to Ulster opinion, as the popular campaign grew ever more shrill. But any concession to unionism would be resisted by Redmond and the Nationalist party. Indeed, part of the problem that now arose from trying to reconcile the irreconcilable was the steady erosion of Redmond's (and by extension, the party's) authority among nationalists, as they were seen to give ground on the original 1912 proposals in order to placate the unionists and the British.

The Ulster Volunteer Force
Although the bill did eventually complete its parliamentary course, by then the whole focus had shifted from Westminster. In January 1913, just as the Home Rule bill was moving from the Commons to the Lords, the Ulster Volunteer Force was formed by the UUC. It was a local militia designed to resist the implementation of home rule when it passed into law. It had the support of leading Conservatives in England, many of whom sent cash. Top military men offered their assistance. The UVF soon comprised 100,000 men and drilled quite openly: drilling was legal only if approved by two magistrates and was conducted for a legal purpose. The magistrates were seldom a problem, being sympathetic, while the government turned a blind eye to the blatant illegality. The Conservative opposition was in effect giving its support to a treasonable conspiracy in support of the constitution.

The extent of the government's problem was seen in March

1914. Fearing that the UVF might raid arms depots, it instructed the commander-in-chief of the army in Ireland, General Paget, to prepare plans to frustrate any such attempt. Paget foolishly let it be known that officers with an Ulster connection would not be obliged to take part in the action, but this merely prompted 56 other officers at the Curragh Military Camp in Co. Kildare to resign their commissions rather than move against Ulster. The shambles is sometimes called the Curragh Incident rather than the more traditional Curragh Mutiny, but the stronger term seems the fairer one, since the net effect was that the British government could no longer rely on the British army to act as an instrument of its will. For the first time since 1688, barrack-room politics had proved decisive.

In fact, the UVF had no need to raid arms depots, because in the following month they successfully landed 25,000 rifles and 1 million rounds of ammunition at three east Ulster ports, of which the Larne shipment was the biggest. The ease with which this was done and the fact that it was organised by the UUC, whose head was Edward Carson, a former solicitor-general of England, and whose principal organiser, James Craig, was a Conservative MP, demonstrated that unionism was prepared to stop at nothing in its defiance of parliament.

James Craig

A last-ditch attempt to find some compromise between nationalist demands and unionist resistance came in July 1914, at the Buckingham Palace Conference, at which all parties were represented. But there was no magic formula. Irresistible force had met immovable object. There was no solution.

Then the Great War broke out. The Irish question was parked. Home rule was enacted in September 1914 but with its provisions suspended until the war was over. By then, the whole world was changed and Ireland with it. Home rule was dead.

The Irish Volunteers

In November 1913, a group of advanced nationalists in Dublin formed the Irish Volunteers in conscious imitation of the UVF. The principal founder, Eoin Mac Néill, who had also founded the Gaelic League twenty years earlier, became its first commander-in-chief. Redmond was alarmed at the thought of a nationalist militia outside his control and quickly moved to tame it. He succeeded – or thought he had – by having his nominees take over the executive committee. But the Volunteers also proved of interest to the Fenians, who after many years of drift had been revived by Thomas J. Clarke, a veteran of the dynamite campaign of the 1880s who had served 15 years in prison.

Redmond's lack of real control was evident in the Howth gun-running of July 1914, when arms for the Irish Volunteers were landed in broad daylight at Howth, on the northern arm of Dublin Bay. This was a nationalist response to the Larne gun-running and, like it, was a publicity stunt. However, whereas Larne went off smoothly thanks to the collusion of the authorities, Howth ended in tragedy. Troops tried with little success to dispossess the Volunteers of their arms; the word of this failure spread, much to the merriment of the citizenry; and when a crowd of people in the city centre later taunted some British troops, things reached the point where the troops fired on the unarmed crowd, killing three of them. The contrast with Larne could hardly have been greater.

A month later, the outbreak of the Great War presented Redmond with a dilemma. Home rule was about to become law and now the United Kingdom, of which Ireland was and would remain a part under home rule, was at war. Redmond

Landing guns for the Irish Volunteers at Howth

committed the Volunteers to the British war effort, thus splitting the movement. About 160,000 followed his call and re-constituted themselves as the National Volunteers. Many Irishmen went to fight on all fronts in the war. They fought honourably according to their lights and those of their political leaders. About 30,000 died. The survivors would return to a country transformed, one where their courage in the face of the Great War's horrors often counted for next to nothing.

'Ireland unfree shall never be at peace'
The minority who dissented from Redmond's decision included Mac Néill and the other original founders. They numbered about 12,000 and retained the name Irish Volunteers. But gradually it was not the formal leadership of the Volunteers who made the running, but a secret Fenian cabal. The IRB formed a military council of its own and infiltrated the inner command structure of the Irish Volunteers. Clarke and his young lieutenants like Seán MacDermott were set on a military action

against British rule, a determination to assert the Irish republic in arms, before the end of the Great War. The IRB were therefore a minority of a minority, the most militant, doctrinaire and unyielding republican separatists in the nationalist tradition.

Their plans for a rising were laid in secret, unknown to Mac Néill and the Volunteer leadership. The only other group in their confidence was the tiny Irish Citizen Army. This was a trade union militia founded some weeks before the Volunteers themselves. Their original purpose had been to protect members of the Irish Transport & General Workers' Union (ITGWU) from the brutal attentions of the Dublin Metropolitan Police during the Lockout of 1913.

The Lockout – the greatest labour dispute in Irish history – arose from a collision of wills between William Martin Murphy, business tycoon and former Nationalist party MP, and James Larkin, the messianic labour leader who had mobilised the unskilled labourers of the Dublin slums. Living conditions for the lower working class of Dublin were among the worst in Europe, crowded in enormous numbers into rotting tenements in what had once been elegant Georgian town houses now gone to ruin and filth. Murphy, the most powerful employer in the city, locked out workers in his transport company for refusing to give up their membership of the ITGWU, led by Larkin. The dispute spread across the city with other lockouts and sympathetic strikes and at its height about 25,000 men were out. The dispute dragged on into early 1914, by which time the workers were effectively starved back on the employers' terms. But in the meantime, the Citizen Army had come into being.

Its leader was James Connolly, who replaced Larkin as head of the ITGWU at the end of the lockout. Connolly was both socialist and Irish nationalist, an unusual combination. Most nationalists, even the advanced types in Sinn Féin or the Volunteers, were either cool about labour or downright hostile to it. The hostility reflected the *petit bourgeois* origins of many nationalists and also their concern to build up indigenous Irish commerce and industry: trade unions, in their eyes, were divisive nationally and destructive economically.

Connolly, on the other hand, was unusual in his context. Most socialists were instinctive internationalists, viewing nationalism as a reactionary form of manipulation by ruling classes. Any appeal to class solidarity was bound to offend calls for national solidarity. So Connolly's combination of socialist and nationalist conviction required a considerable amount of intellectual gymnastics to justify it.

James Connolly

The net effect was, however, that he found himself possessed of his own small militia in the form of the Citizen Army. He was a fine organiser, a practical man of action and a dedicated revolutionary. He wanted to ally himself with the Volunteers but feared that the leadership was too timid. In fact, there were three broad elements in the Irish Volunteers. The first, the non-IRB element under Mac Néill, were separatists who were prepared to resist the introduction of conscription in Ireland. The second were the mainstream IRB members, who were anxious for a rising and sought to build public opinion in support of such a course. Finally, there were the *enragés* on the military council who wanted a rising as soon as possible without waiting for public opinion.

It was to this group that Connolly attached himself, largely through his growing friendship with Patrick Pearse, the most public of them. A well-known teacher and journalist and a brilliant orator, Pearse had delivered a spell-binding oration at the graveside of the old Fenian Jeremiah O'Donovan Rossa in August 1915 which ended with the peroration about the British rulers of Ireland: 'The fools, the fools, the fools! – they have left us our Fenian dead, and while Ireland holds these graves, Ireland unfree shall never be at peace.'

There were soon to be more dead and more graves.

The 1916 Rising

The rising of 1916 was planned in secret by the military council of the IRB and the Irish Citizen Army. IRB people not on the military council were kept in the dark, not to mention the mainstream leadership of the Irish Volunteers. In effect, the military council used the structure of the Volunteers to trip off a rebellion that no one except them wanted at that time. Theirs was pure, unadulterated Fenian ideology: the use of military force to achieve an independent Irish republic.

The principal IRB planners were Thomas Clarke and Seán MacDermott, assisted in the latter stages by James Connolly. Pearse was to be the public voice of the rising: he drafted the proclamation of the republic, although with a significant contribution from Connolly. The vital business of procuring arms was entrusted to Sir Roger Casement.

Casement was originally from Co. Antrim. Born into a prosperous Protestant family, he entered the British colonial service in 1892, apparently a perfectly conventional young man of his time and place. He was anything but: he was homosexual; a naturalist who acquired an international reputation; a humanitarian. In 1904, he wrote a report that exposed the horrific treatment of indigenous workers in the Belgian Congo. In 1912, he published a similar report on the workers' conditions along the Putamayo river in Peru. Both reports created a sensation in Europe, exposing the dirty underbelly of imperialism. In the same year, Casement retired from the colonial service with a knighthood, but also with a distaste for imperialism in general that was now focused on his homeland.

He had become a committed Irish nationalist. He joined the Volunteers and spent the first part of the Great War in Berlin, trying to persuade Irish prisoners-of-war to form an Irish brigade to fight in a rising. He had little success. But his German contacts proved valuable in arms procurement. And so, in April 1916, Casement watched as a cargo ship, the *Aud*, was loaded with arms to be landed in Ireland for use in the military council's rising now planned for Easter Sunday. There were 20,000 rifles, 1 million rounds of ammunition and ten machine guns, mostly captured from the Russians at the battle of Tannenberg in 1914. The *Aud* set sail, followed closely by a submarine in which Casement travelled. They were bound for Tralee Bay in Co. Kerry.

The *Aud* got there first but was intercepted by the Royal Navy. Its captain scuttled the ship and the military council's longed-for arms shipment went to Davy Jones's locker. The submarine bearing Casement and his companions arrived later; they were put ashore, but Casement was captured. It was Good Friday, two days before the rising was due to be launched.

The British authorities in Dublin Castle had known that something was up but were not sure what. Now they felt that they could relax. They were almost as surprised by the turn of events as the Volunteer leadership. Realising the extent of the deception used to get things to this point, Mac Néill ordered that all Volunteer movements and exercises over the Easter weekend were to be halted. The order was couriered to the provinces and also carried in the *Sunday Independent* newspaper.

The military council resolved to go ahead anyway. Despite all the confusion, they were determined on a gesture. The Easter Rising was the politics of theatre.

On Easter Monday morning, a group of 150 men occupied the General Post Office in Sackville (now O'Connell) Street in Dublin. On the steps, Patrick Pearse stepped forward to read the proclamation of the republic, one of the most quoted documents in Irish history, to a bemused audience of citizens. A further six rebel garrisons were established at other positions around the city centre. The British, taken utterly by surprise, mobilised troops from the Curragh camp, about thirty-five miles away, and moved them to Dublin. They began to throw a cordon around the city centre, trapping the various rebel garrisons within. On the Wednesday, they sailed the gunboat *Helga* up the river and used her guns to flatten Liberty Hall – Connolly's trade union headquarters. Troops entered Trinity College and the Shelbourne Hotel, giving them respectively a clear line of fire towards the GPO in Sackville Street and the garrison in the Royal College of Surgeons on the west side of St Stephen's Green.

In general, the rebel tactics were naïve to non-existent. They fortified certain public buildings and dug in, inviting the inevitable British counter-attack. The rebels, with their tiny numbers, fought well. An outpost of the Boland's Mills garrison, on the south-eastern flank, ambushed reinforcements shipped in from Britain as they marched into the city, inflicting the heaviest crown casualties of Easter Week. It was a ferocious fight conducted by seven young rebels and it left over 200 crown troops dead. But despite episodes such as this, there could only be one military outcome. No one was in any doubt on that score.

'All changed, changed utterly'

The main counter-attack on the GPO took place on Friday and Saturday, culminating in the evacuation of the building. The final surrender came at 2.30 pm on the Saturday. The rebels were rounded up and imprisoned. A military court was established to try them and by the time it had finished its work, fifteen leaders of the rising – including all seven signatories of the proclamation – had been shot. Connolly was the last of them. Wounded in the rising, he was tied to a chair and executed. The final *coda* came with the hanging of Roger Casement in August on a charge of treason.

At first, public opinion was indifferent or hostile to the rising. Gradually, anger set in as the gruesome series of executions continued. The British made martyrs of the leaders. The novelist James Stephens, who kept a diary of Easter Week, noted contemporaneously: 'The truth is that Ireland is not cowed. She is excited a little. ... She was not with the revolution, but in a few months she will be, and her heart which was withering will

The GPO in ruins after the Rising

be warmed by the knowledge that men thought her worth dying for.'

Stephens was right. The Easter Rising transformed Ireland. The British called it the Sinn Féin rebellion, although Sinn Féin had nothing to do with it. None the less, it was the Sinn Féin party which now became the focus of all those who celebrated the rising and were weary of Redmond. The party reconstituted itself in 1917. The founder, Arthur Griffith, stood aside to allow the leadership to pass to the most senior surviving garrison commander from the rising, Eamon de Valera.

The war of independence
Sinn Féin fought three by-elections against the Nationalist party, winning them all, and then annihilating the party in the 1918 general election to become the undisputed voice of nationalist Ireland. Pledged not to take their seats at Westminster, they constituted themselves as Dáil Éireann, the assembly of Ireland, meeting for the first time on 21 January 1919. On the same day, two unarmed policemen were shot dead in an ambush in Co. Tipperary in what was the first action of the Irish war of independence.

This war was prosecuted by the Irish Republican Army (IRA), as the Volunteers now styled themselves. It was series of sporadic regional guerrilla conflicts, depending on the initiative of vigorous and committed local commanders. It was an ambush war, directed in the first place at the isolated barracks of the Royal Irish Constabulary. By forcing the RIC from large parts of the countryside, the IRA weakened the local eyes and ears of British rule in rural Ireland.

The infamous Black and Tans

The British responded with a mixture of regular troops and auxiliaries, the infamous Black and Tans. It was a dirty war. The Black and Tans were ill-disciplined and often drunk. Many were rootless veterans of the western front, brutalised by their experiences. They were terrifying when they ran amok, as they did in Cork city centre and in the little town of Balbriggan, just north of Dublin, both of which they burned to the ground. The IRA had a number of successful ambush battles against crown troops, especially in Co. Cork: the actions at Crossbarry and Kilmichael were particularly celebrated. Equally, however, the Cork campaign took a sectarian turn and a number of atrocities were committed against local Protestants. The new republic carried some antique baggage.

The military campaign was paralleled by a civil one. Sinn Féin established the rudiments of an alternative civil administration to the British, complete with a department of finance to raise loans, a very successful alternative court system to adjudicate local disputes and a vigorous propaganda arm. The key figure was Michael Collins.

Not yet 30, this extraordinary force of nature was simultaneously Minister of Finance in the alternative administration, where he successfully administered the raising of Dáil loans both in Ireland and the United States, and director of intelligence of the IRA, in which role he ruthlessly infiltrated and damaged the British security system in Dublin Castle. Collins was prepared to play very dirty indeed, as he showed on the morning of Bloody Sunday, 21 November 1920, when his men executed eleven British agents in their beds in cold blood. In retaliation, a party of Auxiliaries killed twelve people in Croke Park, the Dublin headquarters of the GAA, when they fired into the crowd during a football game that afternoon.

Partition

The war was fought to a stalemate by the summer of 1921. By then, the island had been partitioned. The Government of Ireland Act 1920 – successor to the ill-fated Home Rule Act of 1914 that never saw the light of day – bowed to the inevitable. Ulster could not be coerced into a nationalist state. So the 1920 act created two parliaments, one for the six most Protestant

'Men of the South', a painting by Seán Keating, depicts the War of Independence

counties of Ulster, and one for the rest of the country. The northern parliament began to function and lasted until 1972. The southern parliament was still-born, bypassed by the Dáil.

The birth of Northern Ireland was accompanied by an orgy of sectarian violence in the years 1920–22. The war of independence spread north and became entangled with the trauma of partition. The IRA attacked police and army as in the south; Protestant mobs drove Catholic workers from the Belfast shipyards; the IRA retaliated by burning businesses and big houses in rural Ulster to try to take the pressure off their beleaguered co-religionists in Belfast; the UVF was re-formed as the Ulster Special Constabulary – the notorious B Specials – a viciously partisan Protestant militia; sixty-one people died in Belfast alone in the single month of March 1922.

In essence, the sectarian civil war that had been postponed by the outbreak of the Great War had now broken out in the Ulster cockpit. Inevitably, given the local superiority of Protestant numbers and the fact that they now controlled the levers of the state, the Protestants were able to bring a greater terror to bear than the Catholics. That said, it is not simply an exercise in even-handedness to state that atrocities were committed on both sides. It was not all one-way traffic. But the Protestant traffic was not just more lethal; it polluted its own community, as well as terrorising the Catholic one, by permitting the agents of the newly partitioned state literally to get away with murder.

The treaty

The IRA's war of independence ended with a truce in July 1921. Negotiations between the Sinn Féin leadership and the British began in October and culminated in a treaty proposal on 6 December. It gave southern Ireland effective independence, along the same lines as Canada, but retained the oath of allegiance to the crown and therefore stopped short of a republic. The principal Irish negotiators were Griffith and Collins. De Valera, the political leader of Irish nationalism and the most subtle negotiating intellect, stayed at home. This was ostensibly to prepare the people for the inevitable compromise solution to come.

Michael Collins

It was all the more surprising then that de Valera himself was one of the first to repudiate the terms of the treaty. After the heady five years of republican expectation since the rising, there was bound to be some degree of disappointment. None the less, the Dáil approved the treaty by a narrow margin. There followed an uneasy few months before dissidents in the IRA occupied the Four Courts in Dublin. Collins, by now chairman of the provisional government in charge of southern Ireland until the civil authorities of the Irish Free State set up by the terms of the treaty could take over, was pressurised by the British into rooting them out. This he did, in June 1922, using field guns.

This action tripped off the civil war. It was bitter, as all these things are, but the government held all the big cards. There was little resistance outside Munster and by April 1923 it was over. But it claimed the lives of Griffith – from a stroke – and Collins, from a sniper's bullet in his native Co. Cork. In the meantime, the Irish Free State had been born in December 1922. The last British troops left, as did the last British officials. The union flag came down and the tricolour flag first introduced by the Young Irelanders 74 years earlier flew on all public buildings.

There were now two states in Ireland. In the south, the Irish Free State was effectively an independent country. It was overwhelmingly Catholic. In the six counties of the north-east, Northern Ireland was an autonomous province within the United Kingdom. It had a population that was roughly two-thirds Protestant, but with a Catholic minority inflexibly opposed to the very existence of the state.

10
THE BIG SLEEP

The Free State

After the end of the civil war, the Irish Free State got down to business. Its governing party, Cumann na nGaedheal, comprised those in Sinn Féin who supported the treaty settlement. Its leader, now that Griffith and Collins were dead, was W.T. Cosgrave, an uncharismatic man who had fought in 1916. The dominant figure in the first five years of the government was the brilliant but authoritarian Kevin O'Higgins, the Minister for Home Affairs. Eoin Mac Néill was Minister for Education. Like Cosgrave, four other ministers had fought in 1916.

The opposition – the political opponents of the treaty – retained the name Sinn Féin. They refused to take their seats in the Dáil and remained outside formal politics until 1927. In effect, this gave Cumann na nGaedheal a clear parliamentary run. They could concentrate on government and neglect politics.

The principal achievement of Cosgrave's government during its ten years in office was the establishment of the institutions of the new state. It fought the civil war ruthlessly to a definitive conclusion. In the midst of that war, it established the police force of the new state – the Garda Síochána (Guardians of the Peace) – as an unarmed body. This was a remarkable change from British days. Henceforth, policing was to be consensual rather than coercive. The success of this courageous initiative underlined the basic legitimacy of the new state, even in the immediate aftermath of the civil war. There is no doubt that a majority of people in the Free State accepted the treaty settlement, although with varying degrees of enthusiasm.

Economically, the Free State was orthodox and conservative, reflecting its dependence on the powerful civil servants who headed the Department of Finance. The one major economic initiative undertaken by the government was the establishment in 1927 of the Electricity Supply Board and the building of a big hydro-electric generating station on the River Shannon at

Ardnacrusha, near Limerick. This was a departure from orthodoxy, establishing what was a nationalised company in all but name as a monopoly supplier of electricity throughout the state.

A boundary commission established under the terms of the treaty produced no change in the border. This failure – dashing the confident expectations of many nationalists both north and south – reduced the government's prestige and ended the political career of the hapless Eoin Mac Néill, who had been the Free State's representative on the commission.

Cumann na nGaedheal consciously embraced the support of members of the old southern unionist establishment, which further compromised them in the eyes of their opponents. They also drew the remnants of the Redmondite tradition to themselves. They were consciously the creators and guardians of the institutions of the state, but in pursuing this obsession with institutions they neglected the sinews of ordinary politics.

None of this mattered until 1926, because there was no substantial opposition to Cumann na nGaedheal. But in that year Eamon de Valera failed to persuade Sinn Féin to abandon its policy of abstention if the oath of allegiance were to be removed. He immediately left Sinn Féin and established Fianna Fáil (the soldiers of destiny). Still abstentionist, the new party gave notice of its potential by winning 26 per cent of the poll and 44 seats in the general election of June 1927.

The next month, the government's best intellect and most commanding personality, Kevin O'Higgins, was murdered by IRA dissidents. He had never been forgiven for being the hard man in the civil war cabinet. His death moved the government to propose a bill obliging all Dáil candidates to swear that they would take the oath of allegiance if elected. This presented de Valera with an acute dilemma. Fianna Fáil deputies would have to take the hated oath or face the same sterile future as Sinn Féin. The whole logic of the break with Sinn Féin pointed towards the need to cut this Gordian knot. Accordingly, de Valera wrestled with his conscience and won – not for the first or last time – declaring the oath to be a mere 'empty formula', a curious conclusion in view of the fact that it had seemed worth a civil war just five years earlier.

Cosgrave called a snap election in September. This saw the Fianna Fáil vote increase to 35 per cent and their seat count to 57. Sinn Féin was wiped out as a political force. Fianna Fáil was now clearly the standard bearer of the republican anti-treatyites.

The Shannon Scheme to generate electricity was the new state's first major industrial undertaking

Fianna Fáil, the people's party

De Valera came to power in 1932. His Fianna Fáil party was pledged to fight vigorously against partition and for the reunification of the country; for the revival of the Irish language; for the dismantling of the constitutional arrangements laid down in the treaty; for the break-up of large ranches and the creation of the greatest possible number of small family farms; and for the abandonment of Cumann na nGaedheal's free trade policies in favour of protection and the development of native industry behind tariff barriers.

On the first two policies, Fianna Fáil failed dismally. No Irish nationalists of any kind had a clue what to do about Northern Ireland, except to hurl invective at Ulster unionists. On the language issue, it seemed that the Irish people were as utilitarian as Daniel O'Connell had been a century earlier. The whole propaganda apparatus of the state was directed to the promotion of the language. To no avail: the decline continued inexorably. Irish people voted with their tongues.

On the constitutional front, de Valera was in his element. Half Machiavelli, half sententious Jesuit, he did not hesitate. The crown's representative in the Free State, the governor-general, was effectively fired and replaced by a de Valera crony who barely appeared in public and who by his reticence made a deliberate laughing stock of the office. He abolished the oath of allegiance by legislation in 1933, to the fury of the British. He enacted a new constitution in 1937, replacing that established under the treaty. It was republican in all but name. The governor-general was replaced by a president; a formal territorial claim was made to Northern Ireland; and the 'special position' of the Catholic church was explicitly recognised.

Like Parnell before him, the old Fenian de Valera was making his accommodation with the church. In fact, he was a man of exemplary orthodoxy in religious matters. One of his principal advisers on the constitution was John Charles McQuaid, a cleric of powerful if narrow intellect, soon to be archbishop of Dublin and the dominant figure in the Catholic church at the mid century. De Valera occupied the mainstream of Irish nationalist life in which the church was the supreme arbiter of moral value. Ireland was a country saturated in Catholicism: the unspoken assumption was that the basic integrating force in society was the shared Catholicism of its citizens. Even the GAA, with all its Fenian inheritance, was full of priests. In this context, de Valera's piety was unremarkable. It was perfectly natural that he should express the common moral values of his community.

The ease with which Fianna Fáil had taken over the state apparatus, had amended it in fulfilment of its election promises and had reached a *modus vivendi* with a civil service which it had previously held in suspicion indicated the extent to which a stable political consensus had been established. Fianna Fáil was the party of the nation, a populist, people's party with broad cross-class appeal in the classic tradition of Irish political mobilisation. Cumann na nGaedheal reacted badly to its loss of office, flirting briefly with a neo-fascist group called the Blueshirts before reinventing itself as Fine Gael. It remained preeminently the party of the state, emphasising institutions rather than people; less ruthless about organisation; more high-minded about policy; often wanting for the common touch and appealing disproportionately to large farmers and the upper middle class. Fianna Fáil leaned to the left; Fine Gael was very firmly on the right.

What both parties had was a basic commitment to democracy and the rule of law. There were anti-democratic elements close to both: Fianna Fáil was still indulgent towards the IRA while, as noted above, Fine Gael emerged from an entanglement with the Blueshirts, an organisation of overheated Catholic zealots in search of an Hibernian Mussolini: all they got was an ex-chief of police called O'Duffy. But the remarkable aspect of Ireland in the 1930s was the extent to which fashionable anti-democratic movements *failed* to gain ground.

The drive for self-sufficiency

On the economic front, the promise to develop Irish industry behind tariff barriers was redeemed under the direction of the energetic young Minister for Industry & Commerce, Seán Lemass. The necessary legislation was put in place by the mid-1930s and an experiment in economic self-sufficiency began which would last for a quarter of a century. Fianna Fáil were much more enthusiastic than their predecessors about establishing public enterprises such as the national airline, Aer Lingus, which was founded in 1936.

On the social side, the new government displayed considerable energy in slum clearance and the provision of new suburban public housing. But the crunch came in the countryside, because there was one more election promise to honour which caused a major crisis. De Valera had promised to withhold the annuities due to the British Treasury in repayment of loans extended to tenants under the various land purchase acts, of which Wyndham's Act of 1903 was the best known. He did so. The British retaliated by slapping import duties on Irish produce, of which cattle were the most important. This so-called 'economic war' dragged on until 1938, causing much hardship in an Ireland already feeling the effects of the depression that followed the Wall Street Crash of 1929.

The economic war was finally settled under the terms of the Anglo-Irish agreement of 1938, which also tackled other irritants in Anglo-Irish relations. The annuities were converted into a single lump sum which Dublin paid to London. On the constitutional side, there was much clearing of the air, as the British reconciled themselves to de Valera's neo-republican document of 1937. De Valera also secured the return of three ports which the Royal Navy had retained under the terms of the treaty.

Neutral and poor

When World War II broke out, Dublin demonstrated its independence in the most emphatic way by remaining neutral. In this, it simply did what every other small nation in Europe did if it could get away with it. Public opinion was overwhelmingly for neutrality, although this did not stop significant numbers of volunteers from the south joining the British forces. Nor did it stop elements in the IRA from trying to cosy up to Nazi Germany.

Officially, de Valera maintained a policy of the most scrupulous neutrality. Unofficially, Ireland was neutral for

Eamon de Valera: his presence dominated Ireland for four decades

Britain. Whether out of prudence or conviction, the government showed 'a certain consideration for Britain'. Thus, German airmen shot down over Ireland were promptly interned for the duration of the war. British (or other allied) pilots were slipped across the border into Northern Ireland and no questions asked.

The combination of economic isolation caused by the tariff regime, the inevitable shortages caused by the war, Ireland's geographical remoteness and its aloofness from a conflict that was convulsing the world was enervating. The fizz went out of the government. The reforming impulse that had made the 1930s exciting weakened. The war ended. Europe, boosted by Marshall Aid, produced an astonishing economic recovery in the 1950s in which Ireland did not share. The country was still run for the benefit of a deeply conservative farming class. In effect, the land settlement and the absence of heavy industry had ensured that Ireland's political revolution would be socially conservative.

De Valera was a romantic reactionary. He believed in the moral superiority of the small family farm, of simple rural life over urban life, of an Ireland living as far as possible in seclusion from the world and steering her own course. The net effect of all this was that the Republic of Ireland (the republic had formally been declared in 1949) was the only country in the capitalist world whose economy actually contracted in the post-war years. Over 400,000 persons emigrated in the 1950s alone. The population of the state declined in the first forty years of independence. By the late 1950s, the game was up for social and economic self-sufficiency. This old ideal, which went back to Arthur Griffith's Sinn Féin, had brought the country to its knees.

Apart from de Valera's social vision, one reason why the Republic pursued these policies long after they had anything to offer was that they suited the country's collective self-image. Like many ethnic nationalisms across Europe, there was a distinct anti-modern side to Irish independence. The imperial master represented an intrusive modernism; freedom meant a retreat into a simpler, more traditional moral order. De Valera's vision of domestic frugality and simplicity was reflected in popular attitudes. The rural small holder was regarded as the ideal national type. In many European countries, this kind of sensibility produced fascist movements of one sort or another; in Ireland, at least spared that, it eventually produced a grand stasis.

De Valera was Taoiseach (as the prime minister was called under the 1937 constitution) for all but six years from 1932 to 1959. He dominated Irish life precisely because he embodied the aspirations and ideals of the population. He was tall, austere, commanding. To his political followers, he was simply 'The Chief'. To his enemies he was, in Oliver St John Gogarty's memorable phrase, 'the Spanish onion in the Irish stew'. But no one could deny his command of public opinion, his devious and serpentine intellect, his sincere passion for the Irish language and the republican ideals of the old Sinn Féin. Sadly, he overstayed his welcome by at least ten years.

Catholic Ireland

One other group was entirely pleased with the introverted Ireland of the de Valera years. The Catholic church liked the idea of Ireland as a kind of spiritual *cordon sanitaire* from which the excesses of secular modernity were excluded. The ultramontane church bequeathed by Cardinal Cullen in the nineteenth century was authoritarian, dogmatic and – by 1950 or so – at the height of its influence and prestige. Its moral writ ran with irresistible force.

When the coalition government of 1948-51 – the first non-de Valera administration since 1932 – tried to introduce free medical care for mothers and children under 16, it sparked off a church-state clash which the church won hands down. The sponsoring minister, a left-wing maverick named Noel Browne, was forced to resign. Members of the cabinet wrote to John Charles McQuaid, the archbishop of Dublin and principal opponent of the scheme, in the most fawning and obsequious terms to prove their loyalty. McQuaid's objection was that Catholic social teaching decreed that such services as Browne proposed were the province of the family rather than the state.

It was quite a thing to be a Catholic bishop in Ireland in the mid-twentieth century. It was a guarantee of immense deference and prestige. Catholic Ireland, it seemed, was the last vibrant corner of the Victorian world. Religious observance and devotion were nearly universal. Almost every Catholic went to

Mass each Sunday; abstention was a social scandal. This was not a church that encouraged theological speculation or internal debate.

The Irish Catholic church also had an enormous missionary presence overseas. In every part of the English-speaking world and in most of Africa, Irish priests, nuns and brothers were to be found. The Irish church regarded its missionary outreach as a spiritual analogue to Britain's material empire and all the more honourable for that. The Irish missionaries did not simply spread the faith; they provided teachers and medical personnel in huge numbers.

At home, the entire education system was denominational – this key ambition of the church had been fulfilled promptly in the 1920s on securing independence. The schools were run by priests, nuns and brothers. The latter, in particular, educated generations of lower-middle class boys who might otherwise have received little or no schooling at all. Still, it was a utilitarian, Gradgrind type of education for the most part – another Victorian survival. And behind the benign and selfless achievements of generations of clerical teachers lay the dark secret of sexual abuse of minors, in schools, orphanages and penal institutions run for the state by religious orders.

The traditional church was obsessed with sex and the sins of the flesh. These were, in a sense, the only real sins. The deep puritanism of the church was partly a further manifestation of an antique world in which Victorian values persisted long after they had been subverted elsewhere. But it was also a psychological prop in the whole post-Famine settlement. The need for marriages to be delayed until farms could be inherited; the wretched celibacy of many who had nothing to inherit and therefore nothing to offer a spouse; the extraordinary prestige in which celibate clergy were held: these were social inventions, designed to stabilise rural society in the post-Famine period. Irish society got the morality it needed. In this as in much else, church and people were one.

Northern Ireland: a sectarian state

Northern Ireland too enjoyed a long sleep from the 1920s to the 1960s. The one part of Ireland that had fought most bitterly

An Orange parade in Portadown in the 1920s

against home rule was the only part to get it. The province's
devolved government was established to suit the convenience of
the local Protestant unionist majority and nobody else. The IRA
had done its best to strangle Northern Ireland at birth. The new
state was born on the back of a military victory for the unionists
in 1922. Nationalists were to be a despised enemy in the eyes of
their new rulers.

   Ulster unionists created a state in their own image and for
their own community. From the first, Northern Ireland was
obsessed with community security. The police were augmented
by the Ulster Special Constabulary (USC, known as the B
Specials), an armed local militia, who were effectively the UVF
in another guise. Many were Great War veterans. Few were
squeamish about violence, a lack of scruple which was in fairness
reciprocated by the IRA. The police and the USC had at their
backs the Special Powers Act, originally enacted in 1922 at the
height of the IRA war to give the state emergency powers. It was
not repealed until 1973. In effect, it gave the Minister of Home
Affairs power to rule by decree. In its indifference to civil
liberties and the normal constitutional checks and balances, it
was unique in the western world.

   Northern Ireland was financially beholden to London and
unable to formulate any economic policy to deal with the
damage done to the local economy in the aftermath of the Wall
Street Crash. Things were so bad in the early 1930s that the

unemployed briefly threw aside their sectarian animosities to form a united front. This moment did not last and 1935 saw the worst sectarian rioting in Belfast since 1922.

World War II brought a temporary revival, as the economy went on a war footing and unemployment was almost eliminated. There was also a generational change in unionism. Craig died in 1940 and was succeeded, not by one of the next generation, but by his near contemporary John Miller Andrews. He retained Craig's old guard but a party revolt in 1943 brought the younger and more energetic Basil Brooke (later to become Lord Brookeborough) to power. This change at the top did not signify any liberalising of sectarian attitudes. Even the shared privations of the war – Belfast was bombed heavily by the *Luftwaffe* in 1941 and hundreds died – did nothing to lessen communal divisions or the essentially sectarian nature of the partitioned statelet.

Both sides were caught in a trap with nowhere to go. Unionist gain could only mean nationalist loss and vice versa. The logic of the nationalist position was as bleak. Unable to challenge the existence of the state and incapable of recognising its legitimacy, its politics were condemned to futility. In local government, where there might be a nationalist majority, unionists ensured their continued dominance through a shameless policy of gerrymandering. Derry was the most notable, but not the only, example of this.

The establishment of the British welfare state after World War II disturbed this pattern. The benefits of the new system – combined with those of the British educational reforms which effectively opened up secondary schooling to all regardless of income – were applied indiscriminately. Some unionist ultras resented this rewarding of treachery, and indeed it was to have devastating consequences for unionism in the late 1960s.

From 1956 to 1962 the IRA conducted a sporadic campaign of bombings, arms raids and ambushes along the border. It was a sad *coda* to this whole period. It was a half-hearted effort which seemed to symbolise the enervated state of militant republicanism. There were many minor actions, but most were contained in west Ulster. There was no mass mobilisation of nationalists. Belfast was almost untouched. Brookeborough introduced internment and locked up as many militants as he could find. Interestingly, de Valera did the same in the Republic: no one was going to out-republican him. In all, twelve IRA men and six policemen died in the border campaign. It was such small beer compared to what was to come.

De Valera retired in 1959, Brookeborough in 1963. The 1960s was to prove the most tumultuous decade since partition on both sides of the border.

11

IRELAND SINCE THE 1960S

New generation

De Valera was succeeded by Seán Lemass. He was the antithesis of his predecessor. He had little charisma and projected the image of a competent technocrat. In fact, he had been the most energetic and intellectually daring of de Valera's ministers. He had put the tariff regime in place in the 1930s and had been its principal sponsor. But in the early 1950s, when it still retained iconic status, he was the first leading figure in Fianna Fáil to question its wisdom.

As Taoiseach from 1959 to 1966, he presided over a startling reversal of policy and fortune. He adopted a plan drawn up by T.K. Whitaker, the secretary of the Department of Finance, which proposed the dismantling of tariff barriers and the introduction of inducements to draw in foreign capital in place of the obviously inadequate levels of domestic private investment. The plan developed into a government programme which mixed Keynesian economics, free trade and economic planning in a balance that was more pragmatic than intellectually coherent. However, it had two great merits. First, by pointing a way out of the mess the country was in, it lifted the sense of deep pessimism that had gripped the Republic in the 1950s. Second, it worked.

The economy grew by almost 20 per cent between 1958 and 1963. Exports grew 35 per cent by value. Although total employment did not increase in the 1960s, it changed its nature. Industrial employment increased to the point where it could absorb the rural surplus. Emigration practically stopped, for the first time since the Famine. The population, which had fallen at every census since the foundation of the state (except for one tiny and insignificant upward blip in 1951), increased successively in 1966 and 1971. By the latter date, it had recovered to the 1926 figure, thus reversing the haemorrhage of a generation.

President John F. Kennedy in Galway, June 1963. He was assassinated five months later.

The point about Irish economic growth in the 1960s is that it was no big deal by international standards. Ireland belatedly hitched a ride on the capitalist post-war boom. Success came from the intelligent application of conventional international wisdom to local circumstances. This habit of borrowing from abroad became increasingly commonplace in the 1960s: television, ecumenism, supermarkets: all made their entry in that decade. The one achievement that had the greatest effect on the future was the introduction of universal, free secondary schooling throughout the state in 1967.

There was a generational change, as the old revolutionaries retired and died. The new men were characterised by a jubilant rejection of pessimism. Some in Fianna Fáil embraced a freebooting form of capitalism that had more than a whiff of third-world new money about it. Others were more deferential towards inherited pieties and correspondingly suspicious of rising stars like Charles Haughey, the most obviously able of the young Turks. A small but important liberal middle class formed which was influential in the media and the universities. Some of them, looking for a political home and failing to find it in the ripsnorting populism of the new Fianna Fáil, preferred the more genteel embrace of a Fine Gael that now found itself pulled between an international liberal wing and its old domestic reactionaries. A similar form of colonisation gripped the Labour party, traditionally a trade union vehicle, which now found that it had some radical chic bourgeoisie aboard.

Northern Ireland: chaos and confrontation

There were great set pieces: John F. Kennedy visited in 1963, just months before his assassination, to embody the material achievements of the post-Famine diaspora. The golden anniversary of the 1916 rising was celebrated with due ceremony. But that anniversary also reintroduced the serpent in the Irish garden: sectarian murder in the north. It was also the fiftieth anniversary of the battle of the Somme, at which the UVF (otherwise the 36th Ulster Division) had suffered appalling casualties. This conjunction of anniversaries across the communal divide resulted in the re-formation of the UVF and the murder of two Catholic men and an elderly Protestant woman (burned to death in her own home in error).

Yet, at the time, this seemed to contemporaries a tragic renewal of the past rather than a pointer to the future. When Brookeborough had stood down in 1963, he had been succeeded by Captain Terence O'Neill, a big-house old Etonian. His more talented rival Brian Faulkner had the misfortune to be middle class rather than landed. Such distinctions still mattered in the antique world of Ulster unionism. O'Neill set a new tone, not quite of liberalism, but at least of cautious accommodation.

The most dramatic *démarche* of O'Neill's premiership came in 1965, when he invited Lemass to visit Belfast. Lemass had been markedly more conciliatory than de Valera on the partition issue: in keeping with his character, he regarded it as a problem to be resolved rather than a fundamental moral issue. He accepted O'Neill's invitation. The two men met in Belfast in January 1965, with O'Neill paying a reciprocal visit to Dublin the following month. Other ministers followed. A North-South tourism committee was established and other cautious forms of cross-border co-operation were explored.

O'Neill was never fully in control of his party or of his people.

In the party, Faulkner resented the manner in which the leadership had been denied him; others on the right objected to any softening of rhetoric towards Catholics and North-South contacts generally. Outside the party, the unionist ultras found a voice in the Rev. Ian Paisley, a dissident Presbyterian ranter. O'Neill sounded pretty pallid compared to the ultra-charismatic Paisley.

In January 1967, the Northern Ireland Civil Rights Association (NICRA) was formed. Its purpose was to fight discrimination on the grounds of equal citizenship. Implicitly, it accepted the position of Northern Ireland within the United Kingdom. The bogey of partition was thrust aside for the moment. The demand was for equal citizenship for all in the UK. This is not to deny that there were many republicans in the NICRA, happy to use it as a front: any lever would do to challenge unionist hegemony.

The Battle of the Bogside, August 1969

On 5 October 1968, the NICRA called a protest march in Derry. The Belfast administration, in the person of the Minister of Home Affairs, banned it. NICRA defied the ban. The RUC batoned the marchers off the streets. But unlike the old days, there were television cameras present. The pictures went round the world. This foetid little corner of the United Kingdom was about to become front page news.

O'Neill called an election to get a new mandate but won only a Pyrrhic victory and resigned in April 1969. His successor was another plummy big-house gent, Major James Chichester-Clark, a nonentity. By the summer, Northern Ireland was ablaze. Months of civil disturbance followed the NICRA march, culminating in wholesale sectarian battles in Derry and Belfast in August. The residents of the Catholic Bogside ghetto in Derry fought the RUC to a standstill over three days. In Belfast, thousands of Catholics and some Protestants were burned out of their homes. Lemass's successor as Taoiseach, Jack Lynch, made a famously ambiguous television speech which might or might not have been a threat to intervene. In the end, it was the British Army that intervened, sent in a by a bemused and unwilling London government to keep the sides apart.

Entry into Europe

The explosion in Northern Ireland took almost everyone by surprise and caused an earthquake in Dublin. A high-level plan to import arms in support of beleaguered northern nationalists was discovered. Lynch sacked two members of his cabinet whom he believed to be implicated, Charles Haughey and the hard-line Donegal republican Neil Blaney. The courts tried them and others alleged to be involved: all were acquitted. The years 1969-72 were the rockiest in the history of Fianna Fáil, as it came face to face with ambiguities of its history. The party's legendary instinct for unity held it together. The moderates around Lynch held the line. Blaney never rejoined the party; Haughey spent most of a decade in the wilderness rebuilding his support. Dublin was sympathetic to nationalist aspirations in Northern Ireland but it drew the line at overtly aiding and abetting the revived IRA.

The Republic joined the European Economic Community (now the EU) in 1972. It was the culmination of a decade of effort and preparation. The European project appealed principally to three groups: those who supported the new free trade economics that had enriched the South; the liberal intelligentsia; and, crucially, the farmers. This group was unconcerned about European idealism or Ireland emerging from behind the British shadow; they were, however, hugely attracted by the Common Agricultural Policy, which contrasted with Britain's cheap food policy and guaranteed prices to producers.

Europe appealed to cool nationalists like Garret FitzGerald, soon to be Foreign Minister. Hot nationalists – the sort of people Lynch had sidelined in 1970 and others even more extreme – were generally opposed, hankering for the old simplicities of Sinn Féin autarky. The new generation of *soi disant* socialists in the Labour Party affected to oppose Europe on the grounds that it was a vast capitalist conspiracy. On examination, such people turned out over time to be bourgeois liberals all along: most revealed their genuine enthusiasm for the EU in due course. Real socialists and ultra nationalists – each out on the far margins of Irish life – continued to be the mainstay of anti-European feeling in Ireland until the development of the Green movement in the 1990s.

Membership of the EU has hugely enriched the Republic of Ireland. Farmers, most obviously, have profited from the grotesquely wasteful Common Agricultural Policy. EU social funds have been generously disbursed to bring the country's social infrastructure up towards continental standards and to aid hitherto neglected regions. Industrial exports found new markets. Inward investment, especially from the United States, expanded, as Ireland provided an anglophone access to European markets. The country's traditional dependence on Britain lessened to the point that Ireland entered the European Monetary System in 1979 although Britain stayed out. It meant breaking the link with sterling that had existed since 1826 (the currency union had survived independence) and reinstating an independent Irish currency. It lasted until the launch of the euro in 2002.

Entry into Europe was, in one sense, an admission of failure. The full aspiration of nationalism – for self-sufficiency and economic autonomy – had faltered. The nationalist adventure that began with O'Connell had either run out of steam or succeeded all too well, depending on how you read it. Going into Europe was abandoning the full nationalist impulse for a kind of benign imperialism. It certainly meant compromising sovereignty, although how much meaning that term has for a small, free-trading economy in a globalised world is open to question. It also re-connected Ireland to continental Europe in a manner not seen since the eighteenth century.

The troubles

When the civil disturbances of 1969 reduced Northern Ireland to anarchy, the words 'IRA: I Ran Away' appeared on gable walls in nationalist areas. The IRA had swung to the left in the 1960s following the failure of the 1956–62 campaign and had come under the influence of a Dublin-based socialist leadership. There was a consequent emphasis on social action and a lack of emphasis on traditional republican concerns. This proved costly when working-class Catholic ghettos came under attack from loyalist mobs, often aided and abetted by police and B Specials. The movement split. The left-wingers formed the Official IRA and the more traditional – and it must be said more practical – elements became the Provisional IRA. The Provos concentrated

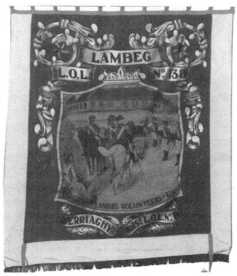

An Orange banner

on community defence in the first instance – to purge the I Ran Away smear – and then moved on to a resumption of the 1920-22 civil war and an attempt to shoot and bomb the British out of Ireland altogether. The Fenian tradition had shrunk to the working-class ghettos of nationalist Northern Ireland, but was still alive and kicking.

Following 1969, the RUC began a rolling series of reforms that, no matter what they did, would never convince nationalists that they were anything other than a sectarian arm of the state. The B Specials were abolished. The local government franchise was reformed to end the sort of gerrymandering that obtained in Derry.

It was too little too late. The Provos were set on their unwinnable war with the British, which they pursued for the best part of thirty years. They did enough, however, to ensure that the British could not defeat them.

The early troubles were enough to secure the resignation of Chichester-Clark and the elevation of Faulkner at last. Faulkner had been Minister of Home Affairs during the 1956-62 campaign and reckoned he knew how to deal with the IRA. In August 1971, he introduced internment. It was a botched job, based in part on faulty and out-of-date security information. But even if it had been a perfect operation, it would have remained a disastrous error of judgment. It massively increased nationalist alienation from the state and support for the Provos, whose operational capacity remained undiminished. The following year, 1972, was the most violent of the troubles, with 470 deaths, over 10,000 shooting incidents and almost 2,000 bomb explosions. In the same year, London closed the Belfast parliament and imposed direct rule.

The Provisional IRA represented the nationalist extreme. The mainstream was represented by the Social Democratic and Labour Party (SDLP) whose principal theoretician was John Hume from Derry. He preached a reconciliation of the two traditions through negotiation and movement towards an agreed future for both parts of Ireland. The SDLP was totally opposed to the violence of the IRA, not to mention the reciprocated assaults from loyalist paramilitaries.

In 1974, the British and Irish governments and the main

Northern Ireland parties reached a deal at Sunningdale, near London, for a power-sharing, devolved government in Belfast. It also proposed a Council of Ireland, which was included at Dublin's insistence and over Faulkner's objections. The Executive was duly set up and lasted a mere five months. A British general election showed Faulkner's party to be badly split on power-sharing, with anti-Faulkner candidates doing best. Any legitimacy the Executive had in unionist eyes now evaporated. It was finally brought down by a general strike a few months later.

The Provos' war

Thereafter, the troubles rumbled on from one atrocity and ambush to another, with dirty tricks on both sides. The deaths of ten republican hunger strikers in 1981 probably represented a psychological low point, although it also alerted the more intelligent people in the IRA and Sinn Féin that while the war could not be lost it could not be won either. Hunger strike candidates won by-elections and demonstrated the potential for political action. It took the best part of twenty years for this potential to transmute into practical politics. The republican movement was steeped in a culture of violence and would require much subtle persuasion to wean it off the gun. There were practical problems, of which the question of paramilitary prisoners was the most pressing (this consideration also affected loyalist groups). In the meantime, the troubles consumed 3,000 lives. The Provos' war – it was theirs, no one else's: they started it and when they stopped, the troubles stopped – grew out of the intolerable sectarian discrimination of the old unionist regime. But it soon acquired an ideological life of its own that went way beyond communal defence.

The most important political development of those years was the Anglo-Irish Agreement of 1985, signed by Margaret Thatcher for the UK and Garret FitzGerald for the Republic. It marked the beginning of a genuine *rapprochement* between Dublin and London and increased co-operation between the two governments. Crucially, it set up a joint ministerial conference supported by a permanent secretariat in Belfast. It stopped short of joint authority but gave Dublin a voice in the governance of Northern Ireland for the first time. Although it led to

Garret FitzGerald and Margaret Thatcher sign the Anglo-Irish Agreement in 1985

predictable unionist rage at a deal done over their heads, it
created the conditions that made the peace process of the late
1990s possible. It also recognised the simple reality that more
than one-third of the population of Northern Ireland had no
loyalty to the state and had no reason to have any such loyalty.

The Tiger's tracks

The Republic mismanaged the economic legacy of the 1960s in
the following decades. It was unlucky in that the world economy
turned down following the oil crises of 1973 and 1979, but
successive governments compounded their ill-luck by gross
economic mismanagement. Charles Haughey staged a
spectacular comeback to seize the leadership of Fianna Fáil and
the office of Taoiseach in 1979, promising to clean things up.
He only made them worse. Garret FitzGerald, by now leader of
Fine Gael, produced his party's best-ever election performance in
1982 which allowed him to form a secure coalition with Labour.
They began the job of rescuing the economy. This process
accelerated on Haughey's return in 1987.

Gradually, the recovery policies worked, helped by the need to
prepare the Irish economy for entry into the single European
currency. Strict EU conditions had to be met. By the mid-1990s,

Ireland had taken advantage of its geographical and linguistic position to become an offshore powerhouse of the American technology boom. It was this, more than anything, that underwrote the stunning economic success story of the Celtic Tiger in the years 1995 to 2001.

By then, a series of public enquiries had revealed a systematic maze of planning corruption and tax evasion among many prominent citizens from the 1960s generation. Haughey himself was the most notable malefactor to be outed: he had lived for years like a prince on money donated by wealthy friends. Likewise, the Catholic Church fell spectacularly from grace, hoist with its own petard: sex. The one sin that mattered in Catholic Ireland came back to haunt it. At first it was almost comic: the bishop of Galway was discovered to have had a mistress in his previous diocese and was the father of a teenage son. He fled abroad. But as the 1990s wore on, a succession of horrifying

C.J. Haughey – twice Taoiseach but ultimately disgraced

revelations emerged of systematic sexual and physical abuse of minors by Catholic clergy and teaching orders. One such scandal brought about the fall of the Fianna Fáil-Labour coalition government in 1994. These scandals accelerated a decline in church attendance that was already visible. More seriously, it compromised the moral authority of the Catholic Church in an unprecedented fashion. Although formal participation rates remained high by international standards, the graph was falling. The Irish Catholic Church at the end of the twentieth century was a sorely troubled and self-doubting institution.

A drift towards peace

As early as 1988, John Hume, the leader of the SDLP and Gerry Adams, president of Sinn Féin, began a series of exploratory talks to see if a pan-nationalist consensus could be reached in Northern Ireland. The SDLP was the dominant group electorally: they out-polled Sinn Féin roughly two to one among nationalist voters. They were famously well-connected in Dublin, Washington and Brussels. It is worth recalling that, all through the troubles, a large majority of nationalists consistently denied electoral support to the political arm of the IRA. The talks were inconclusive at first but were resumed in 1993. They resulted in a document that Hume presented to the Dublin government of Albert Reynolds – Haughey's successor – who thought it sufficiently interesting to begin a *démarche* jointly with the British prime minister, John Major. This led to the Downing Street declaration of December 1993. A document of great subtlety, its essential importance lay in a British acknowledgment that the Irish people were entitled to a self-determination of their own future, thus diluting the claim to absolute sovereignty. The Irish government, for its part, conceded that any steps towards Irish unity could only be taken with the support of a majority in Northern Ireland, thus compromising the territorial claim in the 1937 constitution.

The declaration could not have happened without the Hume-Adams talks or, even more important, without the regular Dublin-London contacts now long established by the Anglo-Irish Agreement of 1985. It led to the IRA ceasefire of August 1994 which lasted until February 1996. The republican drift from violence to politics was painful: Adams demonstrated political skill of the highest order in facilitating the change without splitting the movement.

Modern Ireland at play: fans in Italy at a World Cup match v England in 1990

The drift towards peace eventually produced the Belfast Agreement of 1998, in which all parties – except the Paisleyite unionist ultras but including representatives of Sinn Féin and the two principal loyalist paramilitary groups – reached a nervous accommodation. The bones of the deal were as follows: the union with the UK would remain as long as a majority in Northern Ireland desired it; in return, there would be a devolved power-sharing executive and cross-border institutions to co-operate on matters of mutual concern; paramilitary violence of all sorts was to end; early release of paramilitary prisoners would be a priority.

Séamus Mallon, deputy leader of the SDLP, famously called it 'Sunningdale for slow learners'. Like Sunningdale, it was overwhelmingly endorsed by nationalists while dividing unionist opinion. It required the endorsement of both communities in Northern Ireland and of the electorate in the Republic. Nationalists on both sides of the border did so readily. Ulster unionists showed no such certainty, many of them dismayed by what they regarded as rewarding IRA terrorism. Only a frantic campaign, involving British prime minister Tony Blair, American President Bill Clinton and even Nelson Mandela, produced a wafer-thin unionist consent.

The agreement has held and to that extent the troubles are over. But the inter-communal hatred that divides Protestant and Catholic in Northern Ireland is not. The province is as much a voluntary apartheid society as ever: different housing areas, different schools, different sports, different loyalties. Low-level sectarianism continues unabated, occasionally erupting virulently. Ceasefires or no, paramilitaries still control the ghettos and engage in beatings and knee-cappings of those who incur their displeasure. The distinction between political paramilitarism and gangsterism is not always clear: much of Northern Ireland's black economy and drugs trade flourishes on the ambiguity.

Conclusion

It may be that the period covered in this short history will come to be seen as a distinct phase in the story of human life on the island of Ireland. It was dominated by nationalism – that most modern of ideas – and by the forces that opposed it. Nationalism succeeded wherever there was an overwhelmingly Catholic majority and faltered where there was not. By the end of the twentieth century, the nationalist project had achieved all that it could and, in the republic at least, had re-focused on the nascent federalism of the EU. Perhaps a revived nationalism in Northern Ireland will eventually secure the unity of the island: the demography suggests a Catholic majority some time in the twenty-first century.

But there is more to history than politics, although politics will inevitably occupy most of the space in a short work such as this. The story of modern Ireland has been the story of modernisation itself: sovereignty of people, not princes; democracy not oligarchy; industry and the discipline of factory life; universal education; codification of sports; universal suffrage; the growth of cities; transport and communications revolutions; meritocracy; uniform taxation; efficient sewerage systems and a hundred other things that we take utterly for granted but which did not exist in the 1780s when the history of modern Ireland – indeed of the modern world – began. One could write a history emphasising these things, and mentioning politics only where it can't be helped.

But that is another book, and this one ends here.

INDEX

Dublin Metroplitan Police, 29
Duffy, Charles Gavan, 33, 52

Easter Rising, 1916, 86–90
Emmet, Robert, 16
Encumbered Estates Acts, 45
EU, 111–3

Famine, the, 31, 38–48, *39, 41*,
   74
Faulkner, Brian, 109, 114–5
Fenian Brotherhood, 52–4,
   59–60, 62, 82
Fianna Fáil, 96–9, 108–9, 116
Fine Gael, 98–9, 109, 116
FitzGerald, Garret, 112, 115–6,
   116
FitzGerald, Lord Edward, 8
forty-shilling freeholders, 23–4
French Revolution, 4, *4*, 6, 12

Gaelic Athletic Association, 48,
   74–7, *77*
Gaelic Irish, 2
Gaelic League, 70–72, 74
Garda Síochána, 95
Gladstone, William Ewart, 57–9
   58, 61, 66
Government of Ireland Act 1920,
   91
Gregory, Lady, 43, 72–4
Gregory, Sir William, 43, 74
Griffith, Arthur, 73, 78, 90, 94

Harland and Wolff, 55
Haughey, Charles, 108, 111,
   116–7, *117*
Home Government Association,
   58

home rule, 58–60
Home Rule Act 1914, 91
Home Rule bill, 66, 78, 80
Howth gunrunning, 82, *83*
Humbert, General, 13
Hume, John, 114, 118
Hyde, Douglas, 70–71

Industrial Revolution, 54–5
Invincibles, the, 62
IRB *see* Fenian Brotherhood
Irish Citizens Army, 84–5
Irish civil war, 94
Irish Constabulary, 29
Irish House of Commons, 5, 7
Irish language, 31–2, 70–71
Irish railways, 30–31
Irish Republican Army (IRA),
   90–94, 104–5, 113–5
Irish Volunteers, 82–3
ITGWU, 84

Jackson, William, 7
Jail Journal, 45

Kennedy, John F., *108*, 109
Kickham, Charles, 48
Kilmainham Treaty, 61
Kilwarden, Lord, 16

Land League, 59–62
Larkin, James, 84
Larkin, Michael, 54
Lawless, Honest Jack, 26
Lemass, Seán, 99, 107, 109
Local Government Act 1898, 69
Lockout, the, 84
Lynch, Jack, 111

Mac Néill, Eoin, 70, 83–5, 87, 95–6
MacDermott, Seán, 83–4, 86
Major, John, 118
Mallon, Seamus, 119
Manchester Martyrs, 54
McQuaid, John Charles, 98, 102
Meagher, Thomas Francis, 34
Mitchel, John, 45, 52
Moran, D.P., 73
Murphy, William Martin, 84

National League, 62–3
Nationalist party, 62–5, 69, 78, 80
Neilson, Samuel, 4
New Catholic Association, 23
Newman, Cardinal, 63
NICRA, 110

O'Brien, William Smith, 45–6, 54
O'Connell, Daniel, 18–9, 20, 22–30, 32–5, 43
O'Higgins, Kevin, 95–6
O'Mahony, John, 53
O'Neil, Capt Terence, 109–11
O'Shea, Capt William, 66
O'Shea, Katherine, 66, 68
Old English Catholics, 2, 21
Orange Order, 5–6, 9, 26, 28, 65, 104, 113

Paget, General, 81
Paisley, Rev. Ian, 110
Parnell, Charles Stewart, 27, 59–64, 66–9, 67,
partition, 91–3
Pearse, Patrick, 86–7

Peel, Sir Robert, 24, 28-9, 39
Penal Laws, 14, 19
Phoenix Park Murders, 61–2, 66
Pigott, Richard, 66
Pitt, William, 14
Playboy of the Western World, 73–4
Poor Law Extension Act 1847, 43
Poor Laws, 28, 41–4
Puis IX, Pope, 52

Quakers, 42
Quarter-Acre Clause, 42–3
Queens' Colleges, 35–6

ranchers, 49–50
Redmond, John, 78, 80, 82–3
repeal of the union, 29–30
Reynolds, Albert, 118
rising of 1798, 9–14
rising of 1848, 46
rising of 1916, 86–90
Rossa, Jeremiah O'Donovan, 86
Russell, George (AE), 71-2
Russell, Lord John, 40
Russell, Thomas, 4–5
Russell, William Howard, 42

Salisbury, Lord, 65, 69
Scullabogue massacre, 11
Scully, Denys, 22, 26
SDLP, 114
Sheil, Richard Lalor, 22, 26
Sinn Féin, 78, 89–91, 95–6, 118
Stephens, James, 52-4, 88–9
Synge, J.M., 72–4

Thatcher, Margaret, 115, *116*
The Leader, 73
The Nation, 33–4, 71